THE HOLOCAUST LIBRARY

The Resistance

by

DEBORAH BACHRACH

940.53
Bac

Lucent Books, P.O. Box 289011, San Diego, CA 92198-9011

Books in the Holocaust Library

The Death Camps
The Final Solution
The Nazis
Nazi War Criminals
The Resistance
The Righteous Gentiles
The Survivors

Library of Congress Cataloging-in-Publication Data

Bachrach, Deborah, 1943–
    The resistance / by Deborah Bachrach.
       p. cm. — (The Holocaust library)
    Includes bibliographical references and index.
    Summary: Discusses the efforts of Jews and non-Jews in various countries
to stop the deadly persecution of Germany's Jewish population by the Nazis.
    ISBN 1-56006-092-1 (alk. paper)
    1. Holocaust, Jewish (1939–1945)—Juvenile literature. 2. World War, 1939–1945—
Jewish resistance—Juvenile literature. 3. World War, 1939–1945—Jews—Rescue—
Juvenile literature. 4. Righteous Gentiles in the Holocaust—Juvenile literature.
[1. Holocaust, Jewish (1939–1945) 2. World War, 1939–1945—
Jewish resistance. 3. World War, 1939–1945—Jews—Rescue. 4. Righteous Gentiles
in the Holocaust.] I. Title. II. Series: Holocaust library (San Diego, Calif.)
D804.6.833   1998
940.53'18—dc21   97-26844
                                                                                CIP
                                                                                 AC

Copyright 1998 by Lucent Books, Inc., P.O. Box 289011,
San Diego, CA 92198-9011

To Betty Berman, who is an inspiration to us all

Table of Contents

Foreword

More than eleven million innocent people, mostly Jews but also millions of others deemed "subhuman" by Adolf Hitler such as Gypsies, Russians, and Poles, were murdered by the Germans during World War II. The magnitude and unique horror of the Holocaust continues to make it a focal point in history—not only the history of modern times, but also the entire record of humankind. While the war itself temporarily changed the political landscape, the Holocaust forever changed the way we look at ourselves.

Starting with the European Renaissance in the 1400s, continuing through the Enlightenment of the 1700s, and extending to the Liberalism of the 1800s, philosophers and others developed the idea that people's intellect and reason allowed them to rise above their animal natures and conquer poverty, brutality, warfare, and all manner of evils. Given the will to do so, there was no height to which humanity might not rise. Was not mankind, these people argued, the noblest creation of God—in the words of the Bible, "a little lower than the angels"?

Western Europeans believed so heartily in these concepts that when rumors of mass murders by the Nazis began to emerge, people refused to accept—despite mounting evidence—that such things could take place. Even the Jews who were being deported to the death camps had a hard time believing that they were headed toward extermination. Rational beings, they argued, could

not commit such actions. When the veil of secrecy was finally ripped from the death camps, however, the world recoiled in shock and horror. If humanity was capable of such depravity, what was its true nature? Were humans lower even than animals instead of just beneath the angels?

The perpetration of the Holocaust, so far outside the bounds of society's experience, cried out for explanations. For more than a half century, people have sought them. Thousands of books, diaries, sermons, poems, plays, films, and lectures have been devoted to almost every imaginable aspect of the Holocaust, yet it remains one of the most difficult episodes in history to understand.

Some scholars have explained the Holocaust as a uniquely German event, pointing to the racial supremacy theories of German philosophers, the rigidity of German society, and the tradition of obedience to authority. Others have seen it as a uniquely Jewish phenomenon, the culmination of centuries of anti-Semitism in Christian Europe. Still others have said that the Holocaust was a unique combination of these two factors—a set of circumstances unlikely ever to recur.

Such explanations are comfortable and simple—too simple. The Holocaust was neither a German event nor a Jewish event. It was a human event. The same forces—racism, prejudice, fanaticism—that sent millions to the gas chambers have not disappeared. If anything, they have become more evident. One cannot say, "It can't happen again." On a different scale, it has happened again. More than a million Cambodians were killed between 1974 and 1979 by a Communist government. In 1994 thousands of innocent civilians were murdered in tribal warfare between the Hutu and Tutsi tribes in the African nations of Burundi and Rwanda. Christian Serbs in Bosnia embarked on a program of "ethnic cleansing" in the mid-1990s, seeking to rid the country of Muslims.

The complete answer to the Holocaust has proved elusive. Indeed, it may never be found. The search, however, must continue. As author Elie Wiesel, a survivor of the death camps, wrote, "No one has the right to speak for the dead. . . . Still, the story had to be told. In spite of all risks, all possible misunderstandings. It needed to be told for the sake of our children."

Each book in Lucent Books' seven volume Holocaust Library covers a different topic that reveals the full gamut of human response to the Holocaust. *The Nazis*, *The Final Solution*, *The Death Camps*, and *Nazi War Criminals* focus on the perpetrators of the Holocaust and their plan to eliminate the Jewish people. Volumes on *The Righteous Gentiles*, *The Resistance*, and *The Survivors* reveal that humans are capable of being "the noblest creation of God," able to commit acts of bravery and altruism even in the most terrible circumstances.

History offers a way to interpret and reinterpret the past and an opportunity to alter the future. Lucent Books' topic-centered approach is an ideal introduction for students to study such phenomena as the Holocaust. After all, only by becoming knowledgeable about such atrocities can humanity hope to prevent future crimes from occurring. Although such historical lessons seem clear and unavoidable, as historian Yehuda Bauer wrote, "People seldom learn from history. Can we be an exception?"

Chronology of Events

1933

January 30 Adolf Hitler becomes chancellor of Germany.

1938

November 9–10 *Kristallnacht.*

1939

May 17 British White Paper limits Jewish immigration to Palestine.

September 1 Germany invades Poland; World War II begins.

1940

April 9 Fall of Denmark.

May Fall of the Netherlands.

June 22 Fall of France.

November 16 Warsaw ghetto sealed.

1941

June 22 German troops invade Russia.

December 7 Japan bombs Pearl Harbor; United States declares war on Japan a day later.

December 8 Gassing of Jews begins at Chelmno concentration camp.

1942

July Mass murders in eastern European ghettos; roundup of Jews in France.

July 22–September 12 The great *Aktion* in Warsaw during which 300,000 Jews are sent to Treblinka.

November Germany takes over Vichy France.

1943

January 18 Germans resume roundups at the Warsaw ghetto.

April 18 Beginning of Warsaw ghetto uprising.

May 16 Germans blow up main synagogue in Warsaw.

August 28 Martial law declared in Denmark by German occupation.

September 8 Italy surrenders to Allies; German forces in Italy do not.

October Danes evacuate Danish Jews to Sweden.

1944

January War Relief Board created in United States.

March 19 German troops invade Hungary.

June 6 Allies land in Normandy.

July 9 Raoul Wallenberg arrives in Budapest.

October 15 Arrow Cross government takes control in Hungary.

November 27 Death marches from Hungary end.

1945

January 18 Pest liberated.

February 13 Buda liberated.

April Hitler kills himself in his Berlin bunker; Danish Jews are the first to be freed from Thereisenstadt concentration camps.

1948

May 14 State of Israel is proclaimed in former British Palestine.

Hitler's Objectives

As chancellor of Nazi Germany from 1933 until 1945, Adolf Hitler began World War II to achieve his military objective of world domination. At the same time he waged a war of annihilation against the Jews of Europe.

Hitler lost World War II. The United States, Great Britain, and the Soviet Union destroyed Hitler's dream of establishing a thousand-year Third Reich.

Tragically, however, Hitler almost completely accomplished his second objective. The German chancellor succeeded in institutionalizing murder, killing nearly 6 million European Jewish men, women, and children. This mass murder was driven by Hitler's psychotic obsessions regarding Jews and their putative international power and was made possible because tens of thousands of anti-Semitic accomplices in Germany and throughout Europe were willing to destroy Jews and seize their property.

Almost the entire Jewish population of Europe disappeared, buried in mass graves in eastern Europe or forever lost in the ashes of millions of bodies cremated in concentration camps such as Auschwitz, Sobibor, Majdanek, and Treblinka.

Stifled Warnings

Few people survived long after the brutal deportations from the ghettos and local detention centers to the death camps. So almost no one warned other Jews or the world of the fate of those people who had been and were still being killed.

The Nazis and their henchmen made every effort to keep secret from the world the real and hideous objective of the so-called resettlements. And all too often the handful of people who managed to escape either deportation or the camps themselves were murdered by local anti-Semites who eagerly assisted the Germans in rounding up the few escapees.

Although Hitler lost World War II, he largely succeeded in eliminating the Jewish population of Europe—killing 6 million men, women, and children.

From time to time stories filtered out to the West and to Palestine regarding what was happening to the Jews of Europe. At first, however, these tales of horror were discounted as the exaggerated stories of bereaved people who had been separated from their families. Surely the anti-Semitic ravings of Hitler and his Fascist allies all over Europe could not actually become reality in the middle of the twentieth century?

The Holocaust

The attempt to murder an entire people by another is called genocide. To distinguish the horror, totality, and finality of Hitler's policy from other genocides the annihilation of the Jews during World War II is called the Holocaust.

The scope of the Holocaust is beyond human comprehension. The deliberate slaughter of 6 million innocent human beings in almost inconceivably cruel ways during a five-year period strains belief. In fact, its very enormity has led some people to deny that the mass murders really happened or to downplay the magnitude of the Holocaust.

How Could It Have Happened?

Since the war, others trying to understand the Holocaust have questioned the survivors: Why didn't the Jews defend themselves? Why did the Jews "let" it happen? How could so many people have been killed by so few? And, Why didn't non-Germans help save the Jews?

None of these questions places the Holocaust within its proper context. Adolf Hitler made killing the Jews a national objective: Instead of using Jews to perform military or civil service to contribute to the war effort, he destroyed them. Hitler knowingly sacrificed the needs of his army to complete the destruction of the Jews of Europe. Because this objective was official policy, Hitler's army and police were given free rein to implement it. Indeed, anyone found aiding the Jews could be immediately put to death.

Anti-Semitism

It is also important to understand that many people in Germany and especially in eastern Europe were violently anti-Semitic. This was particularly the case during the period of the worldwide Great Depression of the 1930s. Nationalist leaders exploited and incited anti-Semitism to avoid acknowledging their own inability to deal with the economic crises of the prewar years.

Hitler capitalized on this hatred. He knew that the Jews made easy scapegoats.

The corpses of these starved men represent a small fraction of the many who were tortured and murdered because of their religion.

They were a minority in every country; many were middle-class tradespeople and businessmen. Their visibility in commerce made them easy targets for people who had lost investments, savings, and jobs during the economic crisis of the decade before the war.

Although Hitler had expressed his hatred of Jews in his book *Mein Kampf*, which appeared in 1925, almost no one believed that as the elected chancellor of Germany he would actually kill people. And at first he claimed to want only to force all Jews out of Germany. Vicious anti-Semitic laws passed during the depression drove tens of thousands of Jews out of Germany. The war forced thousands more to try to escape. Even as late as 1940, Hitler's henchmen were trying to make a profit in deals to get Jews to Palestine.

Hitler's plans for the Jews of Germany and of other countries changed as the war progressed. Early German military successes in World War II in both western Europe and eastern Europe delivered millions of Jews into his hands. He had almost absolute control over their lives. What had been an ill-defined plan to rid Germany of its Jews became a well-orchestrated and expertly executed governmental policy to annihilate his victims.

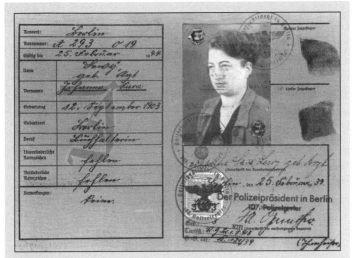

A German passport is imprinted with the letter "J" for Jude *(Jew). Such passports were but one of many measures used by Hitler to isolate and stigmatize the Jews of Europe.*

Sanctioned Genocide

In January 1942 top Nazi officials met to approve this diabolic policy. By then Hitler and his inner circle had determined the Nazi Party knew that they had the ability to exterminate millions of people quickly. Successful experiments with deadly gases conducted during 1941 provided them with the means to do so. At the meeting, just outside of Berlin, called the Wannsee Conference, Reinhard Heydrich spelled out for top Nazi officials the details of what the führer called the Final Solution to the Jewish problem in Europe. Hitler's Final Solution to what he saw as the Jewish problem in Europe was the total destruction of European Jewry.

High Nazi officials knew that it was imperative to keep their intentions secret as long as possible. They certainly wanted no protests or interference from neutral countries. They wanted their victims to be pliant. That is one reason why all newspapers, radios, and telephones were forbidden to the Jews in the ghettos.

So as the Nazis pushed their victims into tightly packed, airless trains, they spoke about "resettlement" in other parts of Europe where there was work available for Jews. The German guards ordered deportees to write postcards to their families, telling their relatives about the reasonable conditions of their new lives. People rounded up for transport were permitted to take along small personal possessions in an effort to make them believe that they would indeed be continuing their lives elsewhere.

Nevertheless, the tens and then hundreds of thousands of Jews who were transported in those crowded, locked trains across Europe were doomed. They were herded into concentration camps built by slave labor. A few joined the laborers' ranks; most were robbed of their belongings, stripped of their clothing, and shorn of their hair, and gassed or shot to death. Gold fillings were pulled from the mouths of victims and then their bodies were burned.

In Poland and Russia, *Einsatzgruppen*, murder squads, followed immediately behind the victorious German armies in 1941. The murder squads rounded up Jews and forced them to dig vast shallow pits. Then the soldiers lined them up, most often naked, in small groups, shot them in the back of the head, and pushed the dead and dying into the mass graves. The pits were covered over with lime in an effort to destroy all evidence of the mass murders by ensuring rapid decomposition. Secrecy had to be maintained at all cost to prevent panic, riots, and publicity.

As German armies invaded and occupied one country after another, they generally could rely on the local anti-Semites to assist them in rounding up and killing Jews. Occasionally it happened that the local population did not want to cooperate with the Germans. Occasionally people resisted efforts to annihilate the Jews.

In those cases the German occupation armies terrorized the populations into complying with German laws regarding the Jews. Those who did not cooperate and were found guilty of hiding or helping a Jew would fall victim to laws that applied to Jews. Reprisals for such humanitarian acts were swift and brutal. Whole families were killed for hiding a Jewish relative or a refugee. Entire villages disappeared as punishment for disobeying German orders.

A Cowed Europe

In understanding the events of these years, it is important to remember that German occupation forces rigorously enforced their will on people from the Atlantic to the Urals, from the Baltic to the Mediterranean Sea. German domination of the European continent was complete. Far beyond requisitioning local civilian food and fuel supplies, as the war ground on the Germans also rounded up local, non-Jewish young people for work in Germany. These people became virtual slaves in German camps and factories in order to fill the vast needs of the German war economy.

Fear, hunger, and a sense of futility filled the lives of most ordinary, defeated, war-weary Europeans. Those who were not anti-Semitic in principle did not have the interest or will to resist the violations of the occupying powers. It was an act of extreme bravery or compassion under these circumstances to defend Jews or, as a Jew, to resist the murderous acts of the occupying powers.

Nor did help come from outside Europe. Even after the Allies received evidence of the Holocaust, they could not or did not act. They were immersed in a global conflict. The outcome of the war was more important than saving Jews in the death clutches of the victorious Germans and their Axis partners.

As the historian Yehuda Bauer writes:

They were fighting a war against an existential threat not only to their political existence but to their culture, their society, and way of life. The issue of the

Jews was completely marginal to these concerns.[1]

The doomed Jews could not hide. Neither could they escape. All borders were closed to the Jews. Secret escape routes were limited. Places of refuge beyond Europe did not exist because the nations of the world closed their borders to them and the British refused to let Jews into Palestine because they needed Arab oil and support in the war against Hitler, and the Arabs did not support Jewish immigration to Palestine.

The Meaning of Resistance

Under these terrible circumstances any resistance to the Holocaust is astonishing. Yet, amid the horrors of war and of human degradation and annihilation, resistance did take place. Many Jews and Gentiles whose humanity rose above their fear and fatigue helped save Jewish lives.

We tend to think of acts of resistance as coordinated effort on a dramatically grand scale: the blowing up of a train, the destruction of an ammunition dump. However, within the hell of Nazi-occupied Europe the smallest act of opposition to the Germans should be seen as resistance. When the German army, SS storm troopers, the Gestapo (secret police), collaborators, and spies were all monitoring one's daily activities, people were in constant danger even as they obeyed the laws of the Nazis.

Therefore, the hiding of a child, the keeping of a diary, the holding of a secret

A Jewish resistance member enters an underground bunker through a tunnel during the Warsaw ghetto uprising.

Major Concentration Camps in Europe 1938–1945

ESTONIA

SWEDEN

North Sea

LATVIA

Baltic Sea

U.S.S.R.

DENMARK

LITHUANIA

EAST PRUSSIA

○ Neuengamme

NETHERLANDS

○ Ravensbrück

○ Treblinka

○ Bergen-Belsen

○ Sachsenhausen-Oranienburg

□ Chelmno

POLAND

GERMANY

□ Sobibor

BELGIUM

○ Buchenwald

□ Majdanek

○ Theresienstadt

□ Auschwitz-Birkenau

□ Belzec

CZECHOSLOVAKIA

○ Dachau   ○ Mauthausen

FRANCE

AUSTRIA

SWITZERLAND

HUNGARY

RUMANIA

○ Large-scale labor camps
□ Large-scale extermination camps

ITALY

Adriatic Sea

YUGOSLAVIA

Mediterranean Sea

BULGARIA

religious service, the very effort to stay alive amidst massive pain and suffering clearly are acts of resistance. All these acts, great and small, are testament to the ability of the human spirit to survive in the face of the most dire adversity and savage depravity.

Most attempts to thwart the Nazis failed. People died in the act of defiance. Many people who were hidden were discov-ered and killed. People who tried to cross the borders into neutral countries were shot. The important thing to remember, however, is that resistance did take place. Yehuda Bauer observes that most acts of resistance resulted in death, but that "The measure of resistance is not its success but its incidence."[2]

Resistance in the Ghettos

The missionaries of Christianity had said in effect: You have no right to live among us as Jews. The secular rulers who followed had proclaimed: You have no right to live among us. The German Nazis at last decreed; You have no right to live.

—Raul Hilberg, *The Destruction of the European Jews*

As Adolf Hitler's victorious armies marched across Europe they changed the social and political landscape of the territory they conquered. They eradicated old political borders between countries. At rifle point, they removed millions of people from the security of their homes.

The Nazis and their Fascist partners forced many newly conquered people to build local concentration camps, prisonlike facilities into which they locked people the Nazis believed were politically, socially, or racially undesirable, primarily Jews. Hundreds of camps existed all over Europe. Many of them were labor camps in which the inmates produced supplies for the German army.

Soon, those same slave laborers built the death camps. These were the concentration camps such as Chelmno, Auschwitz, and Treblinka designed with gas chambers and crematoria that enabled the Nazis to kill perhaps 10 million people in a mechanical and speedy manner and then dispose of their remains.

The Ghettos

Essential to the Nazis' nightmarish vision was the forced evacuation of 6 million Jews from their homes in hundreds of tiny villages,

The Warsaw ghetto in 1939. Jews lived in these ghettos in constant fear as they struggled to obtain enough food and maintain a consistent life for their children.

little towns, midsized cities, and cosmopolitan metropolises all over Europe. The evacuees were crowded into a few large ghettos in order to control and then destroy them. Usually the oldest sections of a city, ghettos were often makeshift arrangements without sanitary facilities or protection from the elements.

Living conditions for ghetto dwellers were unimaginably horrible. An apartment building where formerly twelve families had lived now housed twenty, forty, fifty families, packed together behind the confines of the ghetto walls. Most of them arrived with nothing but a small valise and the clothes on their backs. They had lost livelihoods and homes; many had lost their will.

Whenever possible, ghettos were located close to railroad tracks whose proximity facilitated the transportation of human cargo

Polish Jews are forced to help build a wall that will isolate their ghetto from the rest of the city.

from ghetto to death camp with greatest efficiency. The best known of the Polish ghettos were in the major cities of Warsaw, Lodz, Lvov, and Vilna, where the majority of Polish Jews already lived. There they were joined by German, Austrian, and Czechoslovakian Jews driven eastward to "cleanse" their former countries of their presence. In 1941, in areas where Germany defeated the Soviets and gained control of their land, the Germans also established ghettos.

The wretched refugees who were forced into these ghettos watched as the Germans built brick and mortar walls and wire around them to separate them from other inhabitants. The walls were reinforced by gun emplacements, attack dogs, and tightly guarded checkpoints. Radios, telephones, and telegraph communications all were forbidden on pain of death. Publishing newspapers was illegal.

The Germans took these precautions in order to insure the complete isolation of the inmates of the ghettos from the people living immediately beyond the walls. They also wanted to hide their intentions from the world. It was from these mass ghettos of eastern Europe that the extermination trains rolled to the concentrations camps at the end of 1941 onward.

The *Judenraten*

The Germans established councils in all of the ghettos, called *Judenraten*, generally consisting of the most important members of the local Jewish community. All German orders for the community were issued through the councils. It was the responsibility of the council members to insure that the orders were obeyed.

Sometimes members of the ghetto community offered to serve on a *Judenrat*. More often they were coerced into doing so. Most council members did not live very long: As

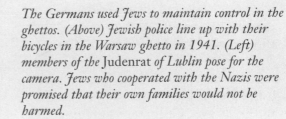

The Germans used Jews to maintain control in the ghettos. (Above) Jewish police line up with their bicycles in the Warsaw ghetto in 1941. (Left) members of the Judenrat of Lublin pose for the camera. Jews who cooperated with the Nazis were promised that their own families would not be harmed.

soon as they refused to carry out the most vicious of Nazis orders, they too, were executed to demonstrate the consequences of disobedience.

Many of the ghettos were policed by a force of Jews from within the community. Persuaded to serve their Nazi masters by promises that their own families would not be harmed, they were almost universally hated by their fellow Jews in the ghettos. When the roundups began for shipment to the death camps, neither policemen nor their families were spared deportation. Many who were not executed by their Nazi masters were killed as traitors by local Jews for carrying out Nazi orders, sometimes brutally.

Terror in the Ghettos

The Germans' use of Jews to enforce their orders was part of their overall sadistic approach toward the Jews. The Germans wanted to drive out all vestiges of humanity so that the residents of the ghettos would follow orders docilely. In the ghettos, Jews were ordered to wear a yellow Star of David to identify them and to prevent any possibility of their being mistaken for "Aryans"; in Nazi parlance, for human beings.

The Germans periodically entered the ghettos to terrorize the inhabitants. As described by historian Israel Gutman:

> The German soldiers throughout the occupation required virtual slave labor. German soldiers in trucks hunted down Jews on the streets to work in barracks, to load trucks, to clear piles of debris, to clean streets. They snatched people with no regard to age, sex or physical condition. The appearance of the soldiers terrorized the ghettos. Men immediately fled from the streets. The ghetto was terrorized by the brutality of the young soldiers who had sadistic leanings or who, inflamed by anti-Jewish propaganda, cut off the long beards of the religious Jews, and taunted workers with continuous shouts and beatings while they worked.[3]

Apart from the physical terror, which made life for the inhabitants of the ghettos a living hell, the Germans systematically reduced or attempted to deny to the ghettos' inhabitants all those things which made life possible. This included food, clothing, shelter, heat, religion, education, culture, and comradeship.

Jews Look Out for Each Other

The Jews lacked the means to fight against this violent anti-Semitism. They were a forgotten minority in a world awash with war and death. They had no international defenders. Even if help was offered it could not be brought in to save the Jews locked away in Hitler's so-called Fortress Europe.

The Jews could only look to themselves. And many of them survived, almost to the end of the war, by adhering to their traditional ways, by enduring suffering and by hoping that life might improve. In the words of historian Lucy Dawidowicz, the Jews survived by following a tradition of defiance which was "devious rather than direct."[4]

In part Jews resorted to this spiritual form of resistance for lack of alternatives. They resisted Hitler's attempt to annihilate them by living as long and as spiritually whole as was possible. As historian Yehuda Bauer suggests, their situation made any other kind of resistance extremely difficult:

> They were isolated from each other, especially in Eastern Europe, by both the Nazis and the largely indifferent or hostile local non-Jewish populations. Annihilation, starvation, the rending apart of families, caused a weakening of the social fabric which made concerted activity difficult. In addition, no government-in-exile supported Jewish resistance, no arms were dropped from the sky, no recognition was given by the Western world to even the possibility of Jewish resistance.[5]

The Jews of the ghettos actually displayed an amazing ability to adapt to adverse circumstances, even when the Germans cut the ghetto inhabitants' daily food supply to less than survival levels. For example, while the average daily intake of Germans in Warsaw in 1941 was approximately twenty-three hundred calories, the Germans reduced the food allocation distributed by the *Judenrat* to 336 calories daily. Ludwig Fischer, German governor of Warsaw, assured his superiors that "privation will deal with the Jews, and the Jewish question will resolve itself in the cemetery."[6]

Many people did die of starvation. In 1941 one-tenth of the Jews in the Warsaw ghetto, 44,630 people, died either from starvation or from disease. In response to the nutritional crisis, the ghetto inhabitants established public food kitchens as they had done for the poor among them before the war. In Warsaw alone 145 public kitchens assisted the destitute and 45 children's kitchens served 135,000 meals, usually soup, daily.

The Art of Smuggling

To supply more food, the Jews became adept smugglers. Small children sneaked outside the perimeter through and under walls and via sewers, returning with bread and other items they hid in their clothing. Although they were beaten if they were caught, the children continued to be a major source of food supply to the ghetto population.

Jews who worked in forced labor camps beyond the walls of the ghettos during the day often managed to bring back food for their starving fellows. Food was smuggled into the ghettos in coffins, in clothing. Whole cows were smuggled into the Warsaw ghetto behind false fronts of dilapidated buildings at the ghetto's edge. People even managed to grow small amounts of food in the ghetto cemeteries.

In fact, smuggling became something of a pastime and even a source of humor for the ghetto inhabitants. In 1942, when the German army was stalled outside important Russian cities, the following joke made the rounds in the Warsaw ghetto:

> Hitler had appealed to the smugglers in the Warsaw ghetto to help him get half a million German soldiers into Moscow. They agreed, but only in their own special way, piece by piece, hands, head, feet each in a separate section, little by little.[7]

Gallows humor aside, the lack of food took a terrible toll, particularly on the weak and elderly, who were among the earliest to succumb. Ghetto physicians were severely hampered in their ability to treat the sick and malnourished; though they established secret clinics when the Nazis closed or destroyed their hospitals, they depended on workers from the outside to smuggle in limited supplies and medicine.

Charity and care for the poor are traditional aspects of Jewish life. Until the very end, the people of the ghettos looked out

Jewish men are plucked randomly from the Warsaw ghetto for deportation to forced labor camps. Such random deportation made life in the ghetto terrifying for its inhabitants.

Sabotage

Many ghetto Jews were compelled to work in war industries for the Germans. Producing goods for the army, however, provided an opportunity for resistance. The workers in the Minsk ghetto, for example, found a way to thwart the German war effort. Yuri Suhl in his article "The Resistance Movement in the Minsk Ghetto," from Michael Marrus's *The Nazi Holocaust*, describes what these resourceful people did.

Many people worked for the Germans in factories producing goods but they were under orders to sabotage everything. As in the Warsaw Ghetto, Jewish tailors working on uniforms for the Wehrmacht sewed them in such a way as to make them impossible to wear; and shoemakers knocked as many nails into the soles of boots as to render them useless. The corrosive liquids they put on leather goods destroyed them and they put chemicals in the alcohol which was sent to the eastern front.

for the most unfortunate among them, although almost everyone in the ghettos was wretchedly poor and hungry. Many people, sometimes the sole survivors of their families, became deranged from their suffering and isolation. Thousands of orphans needed care and the guidance of an adult. Various ghetto organizations undertook to care for these people in a systematic way, as long as

people remained to keep the makeshift organizations in operation.

Janusz Korchak, a famous pediatrician and teacher, oversaw the care of more than two hundred orphans in the Warsaw ghetto. When the roundups began, the doctor marched along with his charges to the assembly point and kept up their spirits by having them wave flags and carry their favorite toys. He stayed with his charges during the train trip to Treblinka and went with them to their deaths in the gas chamber.

The Nazis ordered that education for the ghetto populations cease. All over eastern Europe, this order was ignored. In Warsaw, Lodz, Lvov, Lublin, Vilna, and Krakow, as well as in the tiny ghettos farther east, adults continued educating their children. An active underground library in most ghettos insured that what books were available were shared among thousands of eager students.

There were classes for youngsters in Yiddish, in Polish, and sometimes even in Hebrew. Young Zionists, members of an international political movement aimed at establishing a Jewish homeland in Palestine, wanted to be able to speak Hebrew in preparation for the end of the war when they planned to go to Palestine to farm in kibbutzim, or collective farms.

All kinds of technical instruction was offered to youngsters by skilled workmen, including woodworking, metalworking, and leather tanning. Adults could take classes in nursing, drafting, carpentry, and tool making. In the Warsaw ghetto, the Jews even established a medical school that provided elementary classes in science for those students who expected to complete their medical educations after the war.

Hitler understood that the Jews had always maintained their traditions through organized prayer and the religious education of young people. Both were forbidden. The punishment for disobedience was death. Nevertheless, in scores of basements, attics, and other hidden places, small groups of men met for prayer, for traditional celebration of holidays, and to make certain that their children received from their elders full and complete understanding of Jewish rituals, prayers, songs, and history.

Purim, a holiday commemorating the victory of Jews against their enemy Hamen in ancient Babylonia, took on a unique significance in the ghetto. Parents and community leaders made a special effort to continue the colorful celebration of this holiday, which includes having the children wear costumes and sing songs to celebrate the ancient victory of Queen Esther over the evil Hamen.

Cultural Life Continues

A variety of cultural activities survived in most ghettos despite the horrors of daily existence. There were plays, poetry readings, concerts, and special holiday parties for the children. The orchestra of the Kovno ghetto in Poland was conducted by Misha Hofmelker, who, before the war, had led the Lithuanian opera orchestra. A

Jews in the ghettos tried to continue with their normal routines, even though education and the practice of Judaism were deemed illegal by the Germans. Here, a group of men risks death by holding a clandestine prayer service in the Warsaw ghetto.

twenty-five-man professional symphony orchestra provided concerts in Lodz. There were music lessons for children and recitals in which the young people performed for their proud parents.

People wrote poetry as they tried to understand the meaning of the tragic events that had so devastated their lives. In the Vilna ghetto, twelve-year-old Eva Pikova left behind the following expression of her resistance to her fate:

My heart still beats inside my breast
While friends depart for other worlds.
Perhaps it's better—who can say?—
Than watching this, to die today?

No, no my God we want to live!
Not watch our numbers melt away.
We want to have a better world.
We want to work—we must not die![8]

Humor

Resorting to sardonic, or black, humor has long been a Jewish response to and weapon against oppression and hopelessness. The suffering inhabitants of the various ghettos told mocking stories and sharp-edged jokes to resist despair and boost their spirits. The following story, for example, circulated in the Warsaw ghetto in 1941:

A police officer comes into a Jewish home and wants to confiscate the possessions. The woman cries, pleading that she is a widow and has a child to support. The officer agrees not to take the things, on one condition—that she guess which of his eyes is the artificial one. "The left one," the woman guesses. "How did you know?" he asks. "Because that one has the human look," is her response.[9]

Adolf Hitler and his failure to destroy Russia were favorite targets of Jewish derision. "What's the difference between the sun and Hitler?" asks one mocking riddle. "The sun goes down in the West and Hitler in the East." Or this: A man asks his friend, "So, what's new?" "Didn't you hear?" responds the second man. "Now, they are confiscating chairs from the Jews." "Why are they doing that?" asks the first man. "Because," answers the second, "Hitler got tired of standing outside Moscow and Leningrad."[10]

Isolation, both from the outside world and within the ghetto, was deadly to the spirit. The Jews resisted this form of dehumanization by publishing underground newspapers that helped to maintain a sense of community. People also continued to listen to the world beyond their gates through secret, illegal radios, eagerly following Allied advances.

Ghettos maintained contact with one another through news brought by runners, usually young women who could pass for non-Jews. The runners slipped out of the ghettos, carrying on their persons or in their minds information regarding developments throughout the occupied territories. In this way isolated communities in eastern Europe were nevertheless connected with the outside world.

Jews in the ghettos kept records of their tribulations, resisting the Nazi effort to obliterate all signs of their crimes against humanity. Even if they did not survive the war, Jews all over Europe expressed a desire for the world to know what had happened to them. Perhaps the Germans might be punished. Perhaps some good would come from information regarding their suffering so that humanity would never again perpetrate such crimes.

In Warsaw, an especially intense effort took place to keep records of all events of ghetto life—publications of the secret press, diaries, a daily record of German depredations. For four years, historian and archivist, Emmanuel Ringelblum directed this massive effort to preserve a history of the Warsaw ghetto.

The project was called *Oneg Shabbat*, or Pleasure of the Sabbath. At constant risk to his life, Ringelblum gathered and secreted in various hiding places in the ghetto parts of this unique collection of ghetto literature, a considerable achievement because at various times fifty underground newspapers expressing differing political and religious positions were active in Warsaw. Two-thirds of the materials collected by Ringelblum survived the war. The *Oneg Shabbat* collection lives on as a testament to the enduring will of the ghetto inhabitants to preserve their way of life and to resist dehumanization. Ringelblum himself was killed by the Germans in 1944.

This copy of a Jewish underground leaflet published in the Warsaw ghetto shows Poles and Jews clasping hands through the ghetto walls.

Every Jew Carries a Death Sentence

In an article entitled "Relations Between Poles and Jews During the Second World War," historian Yalkut Moreshet quotes an excerpt from the work of Emmanuel Ringelblum, keeper of the collection of written works produced in the Warsaw ghetto.

Men tore out their hair at the thought that they had stood by while their loved ones, their wives and children, were taken away; children cried out bitterly because they had not resisted when their parents were deported. People swore: "Never again will a German move us from our place without our exacting the price from him. We may die, but the cruel invaders will pay blood for blood. Our fate has been sealed"—they said— "every Jew carries in his pocket a death sentence, issued by the greatest butcher of all times. We must think not of rescue, but of death with honor, with weapons in our hands."

All of these acts of spiritual and practical resistance to the Holocaust enabled doomed people to live in organized, supportive, sometimes religious ways. They gave the ghetto populations the strength to cling to the hope that many of them might yet survive the war.

So they held out, they resisted, they educated their children. Very few people in

In 1950, recently discovered documents of the Oneg Shabbat *archive are examined by members of the Jewish Historical Institute in Warsaw. The documents were hidden in milk cans in the ghetto and uncovered by construction workers in a ruined house.*

the ghettos committed suicide. Many marriages took place. Even a few babies were born, although the Nazis had made birth "illegal." Their fierce determination to live may have led them to resist acknowledging the truth of their destiny, even at the gates of the concentration camps.

Numerous people, even in the death camps themselves, continued to provide support and guidance to those in need, up until the very last moments of their lives. This consolation enabled many people to face death bravely, their final act of resistance to the Holocaust.

Most people in the ghettos resisted Hitler and the Holocaust of the Jews of Europe in the only way they could. They did so through their spirit to survive. As Bauer emphasizes, "Without arms, those condemned to death resisted by maintaining their morale, by refusing to starve to death, by observing their religious and national traditions."[11]

This resistance of the spirit stands as a testament to the inner strength of a condemned people. Or perhaps as Elie Wiesel, a concentration camp survivor, observes, "In those times, one climbed to the summit of humanity by simply remaining human."[12]

The Warsaw Ghetto Uprising

The Warsaw ghetto uprising was the most important and extensive armed exploit carried out by European Jewry under Nazi occupation.
—Leni Yahil, *The Holocaust*

The Warsaw ghetto was sealed by the Germans on November 16, 1940. Until the deportations began in mid-1942, at least a third of a million people lived behind its walls. Although suffering in the ghetto was severe, the Jews cooperated with the Nazi occupation, forming no organized resistance.

Jews tolerated life in the ghetto because, early in the war, the Jews had no reason to believe that Hitler intended to murder them all. When Warsaw's inhabitants learned of mass executions in Vilna, Lithuania, at the end of 1941 they deceived themselves by believing that such barbarity would not take place in Poland. Even when the deportations actually began (each one announced as the last) many people maintained the deception

Many young people in the ghetto questioned German assurances, but were afraid to resist the deportations. The Germans held individuals responsible for the safety of all; disobedience or rebellion by a few could mean the deaths of thousands as punishment. The ghetto dwellers' fear for their families and fellows was a powerful control;

if the young people did not rebel, it was possible that part of the population might live.

Young Jews did not want to make the moral decision to risk so many lives. They wanted proof of German intentions before they acted. They had no arms in any case, and they also knew that if they attacked the Germans before plans for extermination were clear, most Jews in the ghetto, including its leadership, would condemn their actions.

Adam Czerniakow was the Nazi-appointed leader of the Warsaw *Judenrat*. He believed that he protected the lives of the Jews in the ghetto by cooperating with the Germans. He opposed militant action, believing that armed resistance would only further endanger the inhabitants. The issue of collective responsibility weighed heavily upon him, as well. After all, the Germans already had killed hundreds of Jews for a single violent act against a German. Czerniakow continued to hope that a sizable portion of the ghetto population would survive the war. Most families in the ghetto supported Czerniakow. They tried by every means possible to protect their young children and their elderly parents.

Youth Political Organizations

Nevertheless, some groups of politically active, mainly secular Jews, generally in their early twenties, came to believe that the rumors about the mass murders were true. These young people belonged to political parties that ranged from the extreme left to the extreme right that had developed in eastern Europe since the turn of the century, including the Communist, Dror, Hashomer Hatzair, Akiva, and Bund.

Many of the older members of these parties either had fled Poland before 1939 or had been singled out for execution by the Germans in order to eliminate potential leaders of organized resistance. The younger members of the parties, therefore, suddenly inherited positions of leadership in a world gone mad. Despite their inexperience and youth they became the core of the underground resistance to the Germans. In a short time they developed the hardened attitudes and tactics of seasoned guerrilla fighters.

Runners helped the young people keep contact with party members in other parts of Poland by traveling secretly from ghetto to ghetto. The couriers brought news of German *Einsatzgruppen*, so-called special operations details that were essentially murder squads who were killing Russian and Lithuanian Jews as the German army, the Wehrmacht, marched eastward toward the heartland of Russia after June 1941. These were not isolated killings but systematic massacres that took place in scores of towns and villages in the army's wake. Then, in December 1941 and January 1942 news arrived that in a concentration camp called Chelmno, located in central Poland, the Germans had successfully used gas chambers to murder large numbers of Jews.

The members of the various youth groups tried to make plans to defend the people in the Warsaw ghetto. However, coordinated effort was hindered by the same bitter, sometimes irreconcilable political differences among them that had distinguished their prewar relations.

Adhering to the party was tremendously important for these young people. For many of them, loyalty to their parties and comrades replaced family connections they already had lost. Now infighting wasted valuable time.

The Great *Aktion*

Tragic confirmation of the dire predictions of the young people came in July 1942 in the massive evacuation called the great *Aktion*. German troops, assisted by Slovakian and Lithuanian soldiers, surrounded the Warsaw ghetto. Starting on July 22, and continuing for a month and a half, hundreds of thousands of Jews—men, women, and children—were ordered to report to a central gathering place near Mila Street and told they were being "resettled" in the east. From the assembly point, the *Umschlagplatz*, the Germans packed the Jews of Warsaw up to twelve thousand a day, into freight trains. The transports were in fact bound for the Treblinka concentration camp, where their human cargo was murdered.

The roundups were conducted with great brutality. Jewish policemen, hoping to save their own lives and those of their relatives, hustled along frightened families and slow-moving seniors who were terrified by the weapons and dogs that accompanied the German troops.

Adam Czerniakow, saw that he had blindly and mistakenly believed that if he cooperated with the Germans and provided them with money, goods, and workers, they would spare the lives of the Jews of his city. Now he was being asked to help in the deportation process that would lead to the concentration camps and the death of his people. He committed suicide on the eve of the first of the major deportations.

Adam Czerniakow (right) committed suicide after he realized that by cooperating with the Nazis, he had helped them perpetrate the mass deportations and murders of Jews. (Below) A crowd of Jews assembled at the Umschlagplatz, or meeting place, awaits inspection by Jurgen Stroop. Stroop was know to select a certain type of Jewish man out of the group and have him shot.

In his suicide note, Czerniakow admitted that his form of passive resistance in the face of a ferocious enemy had failed. Israel Gutman relates, "Before swallowing a cyanide tablet Czerniakow wrote in his diary, 'The SS wants me to kill children with my own hands.'"[13]

Organization of Resistance

The beginning of the deportations brought together the leaders of several of the most important youth groups. On July 28, 1942, the leaders of Hashomer Hatzair, Dror, and Akiva met to form a united Jewish resistance association. Out of that first meeting emerged the Z.O.B., the Jewish Fighting Organization of the Warsaw ghetto. Leadership roles were filled by Mordechai Anielwicz of Hashomer Hatzair and Yitzhak Zuckerman of Dror, both of whom had been active in underground resistance movements in other ghettos, and Emmanuel Ringelblum.

Determined to defend the remnants of the Warsaw ghetto population, the Z.O.B. vowed to fight the Germans to the death. They believed that for those who remained to fight in the ghetto there was no hope of survival.

In making the decision to revolt, the militant youth groups chose to sacrifice their own lives rather than try to escape through the sewers that ran under the entire city of Warsaw and through which they could have escaped to the other side of the ghetto wall. They chose instead to fight the German army, to inflict what damage they could and to redeem the honor and memory of their lost families and of the entire Jewish people. Yitzhak Zuckerman, also known by the secret army name "Antek," describes the decision to revolt:

> I don't think there is any need to analyze the Uprising in military terms. This was a war of less than a thousand people against a mighty army, and no one doubted how it was likely to turn out. This is not a subject for a study in military school. Not the weapons, not the operations, nor the tactics. If there is a school to study the human spirit, there it should be a major subject. The really important things were inherent in the force shown by Jewish youths, after years of degradation, to rise up against their destroyers, and determine what death they would choose; Treblinka or Uprising. I don't know if there is a standard to measure that.[14]

On July 28, 1942, the Z.O.B. had exactly one gun. But their morale was high. "Becoming a combatant," wrote a member, "meant leaving behind the scramble for one's wretched existence, the sense of being pursued like an

"Our Duty to Die"

Yitzhak Zuckerman was one of the leaders of the Warsaw ghetto uprising, and one of few survivors. Historian Yehuda Bauer, in his *History of the Holocaust*, records an emotion-filled conversation between Zuckerman and members of the youth groups on July 28, 1943, as the great *Aktion* against the Jewish part of Warsaw took place in the streets above their secret meeting place.

> The masses did not believe us. There are no arms, and it seems we will not get any. We have no strength to start anew. The people are being exterminated. Our honor—trampled. This small group can still save it. Let us go out tomorrow into the streets. Let us put fire to the ghetto and attack the Germans with knives. We will die. It is our duty to die. And Israel's honor will have been saved. Days will come and it will be told: this poor nation had youth which saved its honor as best it could.

Yitzhak Zuckerman (right) and his wife, Tzvia Lubetkin.

animal by the Germans, to regain one's humanity and sense of self-esteem."[15]

The young fighters set themselves the task of preparing for the next *Aktion*. Among their first acts was to move against fellow Jews labeled traitors to their own people during the first *Aktion*. The Z.O.B. murdered as many Jewish policemen as they could. Josef Szerynski, the commander of the Jewish police in the ghetto, was to be their first victim. "We don't believe," wrote Yitzhak Zuckerman, "that Jews should lead Jews to death."[16]

After they wounded but failed to kill Szerynski, the Z.O.B. killed Jacob Lejkin, Israel First, and several other men who had worked with the Nazis in gathering Jews for the deportation trains. The Z.O.B. posted placards on the walls of the ghetto announcing to the surviving population that death sentences on these men had been passed and executed by the Z.O.B.

The more important task, however, was to prepare for the coming fight. Obtaining arms was critical. The Z.O.B. central committee sent Yitzhak Zuckerman to the non-Jewish side of Warsaw. Zuckerman tried to make contact with the Polish underground, the secret organization also making plans to attack the German invaders.

Many Poles, including many members of the Polish underground, were extremely anti-Semitic. They were reluctant to help the Z.O.B. even though they knew that the remnants of the ghetto population were in immediate danger of deportation. In part, they were afraid that the Jews would fight against the Germans before the Polish underground itself took action against the enemy. Nevertheless, the Polish underground finally did provide some weapons, which Zuckerman was able to smuggle into the ghetto.

What the Z.O.B. could not get from the

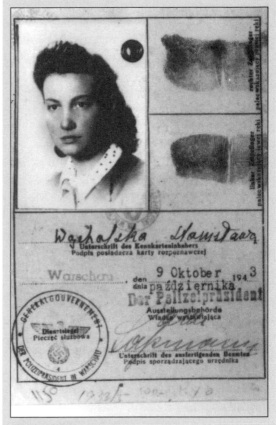

A typical false identification card made for a member of the underground movement who worked outside of the confines of the Warsaw ghetto.

Polish underground it purchased at exorbitant prices on the black market. Members stole some weapons and manufactured crude weapons inside the ghetto. They learned how to make Molotov cocktails, homemade bombs that they planned to hurl at soldiers and at tanks. The young fighters also developed primitive pipe bombs from material they found in abandoned buildings.

Money for these acquisitions and for bribes for the ghetto guards so the fighters could smuggle arms came from several sources. The few people in the ghetto who still had some money contributed. Ringelblum also received some illegal funds from Jewish organizations in the United States. This money from America played a major role in keeping the resistance effort supplied with food and arms.

As they stockpiled weapons, the members of the Z.O.B. also planned the upcoming encounter with the Germans. They trained young people, both men and women, most of them still in their teens, in the use of the few weapons they had. They studied carefully the layout of the ghetto and made arrangements for various groups to defend different sectors in order to maximize the efficiency of the fighters.

Eventually the Z.O.B. formed twenty-two fighting units of various sizes, composed of members of all political parties within the ghetto. Leadership within the units was based on seniority and the squads coordinated their planning and training as they waited for the anticipated attack.

They developed escape routes across rooftops by using ladders that led through the attics of apartment buildings. They could move quickly from location to location without exposing themselves on the streets, where the overpowering force of the German army easily could destroy them.

The resistance fighters separated themselves from any remaining family members. They lived together in small groups, preparing to act quickly when the next German attempt at resettlement came.

In addition to the fighting units, the fifty thousand Jews still living in the Warsaw ghetto vowed to help the resistance oppose the Germans.

Emmanuel Ringelblum, the keeper of the *Oneg Shabbat* archive, as well of the secret American funds, describes the change that overcame the survivors of the 1942 *Aktion*. "We may die," he wrote,

Emmanuel Ringelblum, founder and director of the clandestine archive Oneg Shabbat. *Although Ringelblum and his family hid from the Nazis during the war, on March 7, 1944, they were discovered and shot.*

but the cruel invader will pay blood for blood. Our fate has been sealed—they said—every Jew carries in his pocket a death sentence, issued by the greatest butcher of all times. We must think not of rescue, but of death with honor, with weapons in our hands.[17]

People who had never thought of themselves as fighters joined the underground resistance, undertook training, and prepared to defend themselves. As the Z.O.B. predicted, the Germans would come back to the ghetto to destroy its inhabitants. In 1943, the commander of the SS and police in the Warsaw district, Oberführer von Sammern-Frankenegg received orders from Heinrich Himmler to destroy the remains of the Warsaw ghetto.

January 1943 *Aktion*

Without warning, on January 18, 1943, German troops surrounded the ghetto. Their immediate orders were to gather up eight thousand Jews during the next few days. The resistance fighters, caught unprepared, could not mount a general defense. Instead, individual groups from the Jewish resistance jumped into action.

A handful of young men, for example, mingled with the slowly moving crowds of Jews who responded to the German order to assemble at the deportation center. When the Jews approached the corners of Zamenhof and Niska Streets toward the *Umschlagplatz*, the resistance fighters fired at German soldiers, engaged in hand-to-hand combat, and screamed at the assembled Jews to disperse and hide. Most of the members of this small resistance group were killed that day but they had taken the first overt step against the German enemy.

The Germans were stunned. The Jews had never openly resisted the German army. No German had ever fallen in battle with a Jew.

During the January *Aktion* the Germans succeeded in rounding up about five thousand Jews, four thousand on the first day. The remaining Jews of the Warsaw ghetto went into hiding, resisting the efforts of the Germans to murder them. Another thousand Jews were forcibly dragged from buildings. The January *Aktion* ended after four days. The Germans had failed to round up their quota of Jews.

The Jews remaining in the ghetto underwent a great psychological change. They realized that passively obeying German orders would gain them nothing. The remaining people in the ghetto embraced the Z.O.B.'s attitudes and methods. The Z.O.B. came to "assume responsibility for the fate of the entire community."[18]

For the first time nonfighters refused to respond to the imperious German commands to appear at the *Umschlagplatz* for deportation. Instead, they demonstrated defiant passive resistance. The Warsaw ghetto uprising was the only case during World War II in which the resistance fighters had the active and continuing support of the community for which they fought.

The Jewish nonfighters began to dig themselves into bunkers. Several groups of people got together and designed very elaborate

A Great Yearning for Dignity

Isaac Kowalski, in his *Anthology on Armed Jewish Resistance 1939–1945*, describes the heroic but fatal uprising of the remaining youth of the Warsaw ghetto against the German army.

The fighters knew what they were doing when they attacked the German tanks; this was not a battle in defense of their families and homes because there was no hope of defeating the mighty enemy. It was not a battle for lives of those nearest and dearest, because they had already been slaughtered. Nor was this a battle to save their own lives, for their own lives were already unbearable. The revolt was conceived on a moral plane; a battle for the honor of their people, for the future of their people. It was an act that grew out of the great yearning for dignity.

underground hiding places complete with food supplies, connections to existing water systems, and physician members. The bunkers were disguised so well that the entrances were almost invisible. Many people in the bunkers still hoped that they would find a way to survive.

The resistance fighters of the Z.O.B. knew better. They did not build themselves bunkers, but lived in temporary shelters because their strategy called for sudden movement at short notice. They made no plans for escape.

Between January and April 1943 fewer than a thousand young men and women fighters stepped up their military training for the inevitable return of the Germans. They drilled, they prepared positions, they kept constant lookouts posted near each of the ghetto entrances, and they made every effort to build up their very limited arsenal.

Warsaw Uprising

On April 18, 1943, the Germans returned to the Warsaw ghetto. Two thousand Lithuanian, Ukrainian, and SS troops, heavily armed, wearing body protection and supported by tanks, appeared at the main entrance of the ghetto. The Jews were nowhere to be seen. Cautiously the Germans and their tanks entered the ghetto. Gunfire erupted. One tank was hit by Jewish light arms and put out of action. Under attack at several points, the German force retreated. Haim Frymer, a Jewish fighter, wrote, "We heard the astonished outcry of the Germans, *Juden haven Waffen, Juden haven Waffen*, [the Jews have arms]." [19]

Hitler dismissed von Sammern-Frankenegg for failing to alert him to the possibility of an armed uprising by the Jews. He was replaced by SS general Jurgen

Denying the Holocaust Is Anti-Semitic

The Jews fought the Germans alone. Assistance did not come from the Polish resistance fighters on the Aryan side of the ghetto although Antek (Zuckerman) had made every attempt to obtain arms and other supplies from them. They were abandoned. On March 23, 1943, Mordechai Anielewicz wrote the following letter to Antek, his main representative outside the ghetto. It is taken from Israel Gutman's article quoted in *The Nazi Holocaust: Jewish Resistance to the Holocaust*.

Please inform the authorities in our name that if considerable assistance is not extended immediately, we will regard this as indifference on the part of the "Delegation" and the authorities toward the fate of the Jews of Warsaw. The allocation of weapons without ammunition seems a bitter mockery of our fate and strengthens the assumption that anti-Semitic venom is still strongly present in the ruling circles of Poland, despite the tragic and cruel experience of the past three years. We are not going to try to persuade anyone of our readiness and ability to fight. Since January 18, the Jewish community of Warsaw has been in a state of continuous combat with the invader and his henchmen. Anyone who denies this or doubts it is nothing but a malicious anti-Semite.

Stroop. Stroop kept a diary of the uprising, recording his impressions of the fighting, which extended to the middle of May.

The German troops returned to the ghetto day after day. While the passive resisters kept themselves hidden within their bunkers, the Z.O.B. fired on the Germans from rooftops and building windows. Battles were fierce but brief. The resistance fighters had few weapons and had to make each shot or homemade bomb count.

The Germans had at first expected to wipe out the resistance within a few days and deport the remaining Jews immediately thereafter. Instead the battle for the Warsaw ghetto continued. Stroop discovered the makeshift ladders that allowed the Jews to move from building to building. He had his troops block the passages in the roofs and building attics where the ladders had rested.

He attached listening devices near the basement entrances of buildings to see if his troops could discover the location of underground bunkers. He brought in dogs to sniff out underground hiding places and piles of rubble where survivors might have found space in which to conceal themselves. The Germans were taken completely by surprise by the existence of the bunkers. Stroop made the following entry in his diary:

The number of Jews taken from their houses in the ghetto during the first days was too slight. It turns out that the Jews hid in the sewerage canals and bunkers that were prepared especially for that purpose. During the first days, it was assumed that there were merely a few isolated bunkers, but in the course of the great action it became clear that the entire ghetto is systemically provided with cellars, bunkers and passageways. Each of these passageways and

During the Warsaw ghetto uprising, Jurgen Stroop (third from right) listens while one of his men interrogates two informers.

bunkers has an outlet to the sewerage canals. Hence, this allowed for the undisturbed underground contact. This effective network also served the Jews as a means of escaping to the "Aryan" side of Warsaw. We received constant reports that the Jews were trying to escape through the underground canals."[20]

The Germans began to set fire to the ghetto systematically, house by house, day by day. The fires destroyed the buildings, sucked the air from the bunkers, and severed the water connections that the Jews had created earlier in preparation for the uprising.

The fire and smoke of the burning ghetto could be seen for miles around. Men, women, and children were incinerated in the blaze. Those who survived long enough to stumble out of their bunkers were shot by the Germans. It is reported that not a single bunker was taken intact by the Germans during the uprising.

Jews captured during the Warsaw ghetto uprising are led by German SS troops to be deported. Many ghetto residents chose suicide rather than be captured.

On April 25, Stroop sent a message to his superiors: "If last night what was the ghetto was alight and burning, tonight it is one mighty furnace." But several days later he had to report that "Repeatedly we saw that the Jews and bandits preferred to go back into the fire than to fall into our hands."[21]

Each day resistance to the Germans diminished as the Jewish fighters fell in battle. Each day, the area still under their control contracted. Those few who survived regrouped, each day finding resistance more difficult to sustain.

Finally, on May 8, 1943, the Germans located the center of the Z.O.B. on 18 Mila Street. The Germans closed all entrances to the position and injected poison gas and threw hand grenades into the underground space. The resistance fighters refused to emerge and be taken alive. Soon the Germans heard the sound of gunfire from within as approximately one hundred fighters committed mass suicide.

Destroying the Ghetto

On May 16, 1943, German forces destroyed the main synagogue of the Warsaw ghetto. General Stroop wrote in his diary: "The former Jewish Quarter of Warsaw no longer exists. According to our evidence, the total number of Jews seized and terminated is 50,065."[22]

The Warsaw ghetto uprising ended. No buildings stood intact. Almost all the passive resisters had died in their bunkers or had been killed as they attempted to escape. Most of the fighters were dead. However, for months after, individuals continued to emerge from the ruins of Warsaw.

A handful of resistance fighters, perhaps seventy-five survivors, made their way through the sewers that ran under the ghetto to the area beyond the ghetto walls. Some were killed as they emerged from the sewers. The Germans sprayed bullets at those resistance fighters who had not yet emerged from the sewers. Some actually managed to escape.

So the Warsaw ghetto, home at one time between 1939 and 1943 to well over half a million Jews, ceased to exist. What could not be destroyed, however, was the memory of the uprising itself.

In the words of historian Isaac Kowalski, the resistance had gained a "moral victory of death in battle, rather than in the gas chambers." [23]

According to Kowalski, "The revolt was conceived on a moral plain; a battle for the honor of their people, for the future of their people. It was an act that grew out of the great yearning for human dignity." [24] The handful of young Jewish resistance fighters dispelled the idea that Jews do not fight. News of the uprising spread throughout Europe and gave hope to many others who tried to resist German efforts to murder them. The myth of the indestructibility of the German army suffered a severe blow as a result of the uprising. Many Jews regarded the uprising with honor and held it in the same regard as the heroic battles fought by Jewish bands against Roman legions so many centuries before.

[The Jews] concluded what Machiavelli had long ago argued, that "among other evils, which being unarmed brings you, it causes you to be despised."
—Lucy Dawidowicz,
The War Against the Jews

The Jewish uprising in the Warsaw ghetto was the largest and most dramatic act of Jewish militant defiance against the German army during World War II. It was, however, neither the first nor the only overt resistance by Jews in eastern Europe. What made the events in Warsaw so extraordinary was the fact that the Warsaw fighters knew from the beginning of their revolt that they would not survive.

This was not clearly the case in Jewish communities all over eastern Europe that decided to resist the total extermination of their populations. Unlike in Warsaw, those who resisted there had some faint hope of escaping after the rebellion and of living in the dense forests of eastern Europe and western Russia. The forests gave escapees from the ghettos and work camps a chance for survival. Unlike the Warsaw region of western Poland, eastern Europe and western Russia were heavily forested. People who escaped from the ghettos and work camps had a chance of finding their way to the forests.

Those Jews who lived in Byelorussia might also be lucky enough to find Russian partisan groups in the forests who would help them and take them into their armed bands.

Partisan Bands

The partisan bands were irregular troops who engaged in guerrilla warfare against the Germans behind German lines. In eastern Europe these bands consisted largely of remnants of regular Russian military units that had become trapped in German-held territory following the German invasion of the Soviet Union in June 1941. In 1939 Hitler had made a pact with Joseph Stalin, the Soviet leader, to divide Poland between them and not attack each other.

In 1941 Hitler broke the pact and massive German armies began pouring into Soviet-held Poland, the Soviet Union, and the Baltic states of Estonia, Latvia, and Lithuania. The speed of the German advance caught many people by surprise. Hundreds of thousands of Jews were killed quickly by the *Einsatzgruppen* and many Russian soldiers suddenly found themselves caught behind enemy lines. By December 1941, German armies stood just outside the defensive perimeter of Moscow.

At that time many Jews were serving in the Soviet army. Many of them became

Nazi soldiers move into Russia. The Nazi advance into Russia was swift and surprising to the Russians, who had signed a nonaggression pact with Germany in 1939. Dictator Joseph Stalin's strategy of allying Russia with the Nazis to delay an inevitable invasion was but one of many miscalculations.

prominent in the partisan groups. They knew, as did the Jews in the conquered territory, that if they were captured the Germans would kill them, not take them prisoners of war.

Rumors of activities of partisan groups operating behind German lines came to the small towns and villages where the Jews were trapped. Letters, for example, from Colonel F. Markov, the commander of the Varoshilov partisan unit, and others actually reached the ghettos of Lithuania, calling on young Jews to escape and join them. Soviet Jewish paratroopers who were dropped in advance of their own lines made contact with the Jewish underground of some of the small towns, impressing young Jews who wanted to fight against the Germans and supplying much needed food and guns.

Shalom Cholawski, a survivor of the Nesvizh ghetto in Byelorussia, formerly part of Poland, reports on the spread of rumors in the summer of 1942:

We began to hear of groups of Jews who had succeeded in getting out of towns such as Nesvizh, Kletsk [formerly Polish Kleck], and Lakhovitz, which was situated to the west of the former Polish-Russian border and from Kopyl and Timkovitzi to the east. The groups [escapees from the towns] were heading in the direction of the forests in the Kopyl region. A wave of exterminations swept through these towns in the month of July 1942. Fate seemed to bring the fleeing Jews together. Those coming out of the western ghettos had an intuitive feeling that there were partisans in the region and that they were camped somewhere to the east of the border. Friendly peasants we met pointed the way for us: "Go eastward."[25]

The young Jews of eastern European and Russian towns and villages, just as in Warsaw, did not rebel when the Germans first appeared and enclosed masses of people together in restricted areas. They did not believe that the Germans intended to murder them all. Most people hoped to survive the war. Perhaps most important, they did not want to take personal responsibility for endangering the lives of those people who were not involved in the resistance movements.

Escape to the Forests

So they waited for the right moment to strike. They waited as the Germans relocated the Jews under guard, seized their valuables, and set the young men to hard labor. In the summer of 1942 the Germans began a massive wave of exterminations. On July 22, 1942, two-thirds of the population of Kletsk was taken out beyond the town and shot. The following day the same thing happened to the old, the young, the sick, and the disabled in Nesvizh.

Between the onset of the German occupation in 1941 and the final destruction of many of these towns, furious exchanges took place between those who wanted to

Two partisan groups meet in the forest. In eastern Europe and western Russia, Jews who escaped the Nazis were often able to join such partisan groups to continue to resist Hitler's efforts to destroy the Jews.

How Many Should Die to Avenge the Murdered Children?

Isaac Kowalski's *Anthology of Armed Jewish Resistance 1939-1945* contains a letter written by a fighter in the forests. The letter demonstrates the bitterness and hatred that drove these Russian Jewish partisans and gave purpose to their lives.

Letter of the Red Army Soldier, Gofman (Krasnopolye, Nogilev)

I am going to tell of another tragedy—that of Krasnopolye. Eighteen hundred Jews perished there. My father was among them—my beautiful daughter, my sick son, and my wife. Of all the Jews of Krasnopolye, only one survived—Lida Vysotskaya. It was she who wrote to me about everything. I learned that, a day before the execution—when it was no longer permitted to leave the ghetto—my wife managed to get to town to get dried apples for our sick son. She wore a shameful tag on her chest. She wanted to prolong her son's life—if only for a day. The heart of the unhappy woman beat with love for her son.

On October 20, 1941, the Germans herded everyone together and shot them. The children had been tormented for two months and then shot. My son had been ill for a long time, but the doctors were keeping him alive. Soviet science saved him, and those beasts killed him with a submachine gun.

I am a husband without a wife and a father without children. I am no longer young, but this is my third year in the fight. I have taken revenge and will take revenge. I am the son of a great fatherland, and I am a soldier of the Red Army. I raised my younger brother, and he is fighting now as a lieutenant colonel on the first Ukrainian front. He too is taking revenge. I have seen fields sown with German bodies, but that is not enough. How many of them should die for every murdered child! Whether I am in the forest or in the bunker, the Krasnopolye tragedy is before my eyes. Children died there. In other towns and villages children of all nationalities died. And I swore that I will take revenge as long as my hand can hold a weapon. March 10, 1944.

resist the Germans and those who feared to do so. Generally, young men and women wanted to fight. They gathered whatever weapons they could find, a few firearms, pitchforks, sticks. They planned to defend themselves when the killing squads appeared. They wanted to turn themselves into fighters who would escape to the forests and continue to fight as partisans.

In almost all of the places where rebellions took place, the leaders of the uprisings decided to act only when they believed that the final liquidation of their communities was about to begin. For example, residents of the small town of Pilica in eastern Poland knew in June 1942 that the Germans were about to destroy the remaining population. The head of the *Judenrat*, who had been working with the young ghetto fighters, gave the order that "every able Jew must escape to the forests."[26] A few hundred actually succeeded in making good their escape.

In August 1942, the Jews of Tuczyn (Tuckin, Ukraine) learned that the Germans were digging pits in the nearby forest to be used as mass graves for the Jews of the town. Getzl Schwartzman, the head of the *Judenrat*, organized the people for action.

When the Germans surrounded Tuczyn on September 23, 1942, the people set fire to their homes. Some threw themselves into the flames rather than be captured; those who had weapons fired on the Germans; and others tried to escape to the forests. Most of the people of Tuczyn were killed by the Germans and their Ukrainian assistants. Only several hundred, including Schwartzman's two daughters, escaped to the forests to continue their fight against the German murderers of their families.

In places such as Vilna, where a large number of Jews lived, resistance plans were extremely elaborate. Here, as in Tuczyn, young members of the underground organizations decided to first put up a resistance to the Germans when they came to destroy the Jews. Then, those who survived the uprising in the ghetto would try to escape to the forests. Historian Dov Levin writes that

> The aim of the attack would be to kill and disarm as many Germans as possible and to divert the German forces, thus giving the fighting division in the border areas of the ghetto time to break down the fence, and thus enable the ghetto population to get out. The incendiary division, equipped with Molotov cocktails and other inflammable materials, also had an important task—to set fire to empty houses within and on the Aryan side so when the fighting was at its height the fire would increase the confusion.[27]

When the German attack to deport the survivors of Vilna began on September 1, 1943, the Jewish resistance fighters put their plan into action. Following their initial resistance to the German army, many of the young people succeeded in escaping to the Rudniki forest. They formed a fighting unit under the command of Abba Kovna, one of the young leaders of the Vilna uprising and later a great Israeli poet. These fighters eventually became part of a larger partisan unit, composed mostly of Jews, called the Lithuanian Division.

The largest and most successful escape effort of any town in eastern Europe during World War II occurred in Minsk in Byelorussia. The large Jewish community of Minsk had a very active underground resistance movement and community leaders who assisted their efforts. The goal of the leaders of the resistance movement was to help as many people as possible escape to the forests before the Germans annihilated the community.

The Jews of Minsk established a rather elaborate system for getting people to the camps set up in the forests. Guides directed escapees to the camps and to safe resting places along a thirty-five-mile route. This assistance from people in the countryside made it possible for nearly ten thousand people to escape before the ghetto was liquidated.

Hersh Smolar, a leader of the Minsk underground group, paid tribute to the local villagers:

All who escaped from the Minsk Ghetto to the forest to carry on the armed struggle, and all those who escaped to Byelorussian villages and communities to save their lives, felt at every turn that without the fraternal help of the Byelorussian population not a single Jew would have survived, and thousands did survive. Often they were aided by underground men who helped move some of them on railroads, sometimes hiding them in coal compartments, then delivered them to within a few kilometers of the forests.[28]

It was never an easy decision to leave the ghettos and head for the forests. The mostly young people who made their escape clearly believed that they were doomed to be murdered at the hands of the Germans and that defending the ghetto was hopeless. Many were the sole survivors of families who had been annihilated in earlier deportations or executions; they were filled with a hatred for the Germans and a burning desire for revenge. Others, however, left aged parents and younger siblings who could not survive in the forests and whom they knew they never would see again. Some of the young escapees-turned-fighters left families they hoped would later join them in the forests.

Some of the young people who went to the forests were driven by the urge to redeem the honor of the Jewish people through their own military efforts. Many others, largely Zionists, believed that a remnant of the Jewish people must survive the war in order to establish a Jewish national homeland.

Life in the Forest

Whatever drove them to the forests, however, these young people faced enormous dif-

These young women were members of a Zionist partisan group in Lithuania.

ficulties. Many Jews who fled to the forests never reached their destination. German troops and the bitter climate of northern Europe killed thousands. Most escapees were city dwellers already weakened by deprivation and unable to tolerate the harsh conditions in the forests. And in fact many who came to the forest without a weapon were rejected by partisan groups. As historian Yuri Suhl writes, "The gun was the Jew's passport to the forest."[29]

Historian Dov Levin argues, however, that of all the difficulties escapees faced, anti-Semitism was still the most deadly. He writes that the Lithuanian, Polish, and Byelorussian peasants often turned the partisans over to the

Partisan Forces

Shalom Cholawski was a Jewish partisan fighter during World War II. In the following account, taken from his book *Soldiers from the Ghetto*, Cholawski recounts the important role the Russian partisan forces played in controlling dangerous peasant forces who frequently attacked Jewish partisans.

Bands of Jews wandered about in the surrounding forests searching for a sign of the partisans. The wandering was filled with danger. Many peasants spying on us from the fields would demand payment for their silence. Only in the Soviet zone did we feel safe. . . . A unit of Russian partisans was encamped in Rayuvka. It was made up of local people, Red Army soldiers who were hidden by peasants during the winter, and those who had escaped from prison camps. With the coming of spring they banded together in the forest. They were few in number and poorly armed. After two or three months, the unit increased, and by the time the Jews came in July of that year, there were seventy or eighty in all. It was a small unit, but its territory of influence extended to many villages and towns in the direction of Minsk to the north, to the Polish swamps in the south and to the Naliboki forest on the west. Its combat squads reached distant regions, and as they passed through an area, they created the impression that they were strong and well armed. These units were a constant topic of conversation among the peasants, who would whisper that large Soviet forces were moving about in the area.

Germans. Their anti-Semitism blinded them to the reality that the Jewish partisans fighting Germans in Russian fighting units were their allies. Entire groups of Jewish escapees were killed by the local peasants out of racial hatred and the desire to obtain the guns the Jews had with them. He writes that a "long time elapsed before the peasants learned that a bullet shot by a Jew [against German soldiers] strikes home in the same way as a Russian bullet."[30]

Nevertheless, thousands of Jews were lucky enough to reach the forests with their own arms and locate partisan groups of Byelorussians or Lithuanians willing to accept them. Life in the forest was still full of hardship. Food had to be stolen. Constant relocation was necessary to avoid traps or bands of German forces. The cold winters of the region were followed by springs that created dangerous swamps, making transportation and hunting miserable and dangerous.

Some of the young resistance fighters who went to the forests were fortunate enough to find other Jewish partisans. In this instance, the support of their fellow survivors and coreligionists, as well as the shared determination to kill as many German soldiers as possible, made life in the forest endurable.

Those who fled to the forests nearest the Russian war front were the most fortunate.

The Russian units actively recruited many former ghetto fighters. In addition, regular Russian army officers exercised more control over their men than did the partisan leaders, reducing the likelihood of anti-Semitic violence from their troops. The regular army officers also supplied the Jewish fighters with professional military leaders and supplies.

Jewish Partisan Bands

The Lithuanian Division, the majority of whose members were Jewish, operated in the forests of Narocz and Rudniki near Vilna. In the evenings the fighters sang Jewish and Hebrew folk songs around the fire. Orders to the fighters were passed along in Yiddish. The Jewish partisans said traditional prayers over their fallen comrades and buried their bodies in the prescribed manner, their heads facing toward Jerusalem.

The Jewish partisans also protected the family camps that developed in the forests of eastern Poland and the western Soviet Union. These camps consisted of groups of Jewish people of all ages, sometimes numbering in the hundreds, several as large as two thousand individuals, who were not fighters but who nevertheless had survived the slaughters of the ghettos and had managed to escape to the forests. According to historian Yitzhak Arad the "two largest camps were in the Naliboki forest, the camp headed by Tuvyah Bielski which had approximately twelve hundred persons and the camp under the leadership of Sholomo Zorin, where about eight hundred people found shelter."[31]

They gathered in the forest for security, for comradeship, for hope. They prepared food, mended clothing, and tried to nurse back to health the sick and wounded partisans who did the fighting. In this way people in the family camps earned the protection of the partisans. In general, their safety lay entirely in the ability of the Jewish partisan groups to help them find food, to warn them of danger, and to help move the camps when the enemy approached.

The need to protect the family groups often hindered the activities of the Jewish partisans. They could not always move as quickly or as freely as their non-Jewish comrades. Nevertheless, despite the time they spent defending the family camps, the Jewish partisans provided a good deal of support to anti-German forces operating in northern Europe.

In 1943 the tide of war turned. German forces in northern Europe were beginning to be pushed back by increasingly powerful

Partisans relax in a forest encampment. The partisans protected many Jews who had fled to the forests and formed family camps.

Members of the Russian army. The Russians welcomed the partisans' help against their joint enemy, allowing many of them to join the army's ranks as regular soldiers.

The Jewish fighters in the partisan forces looked forward to the arrival of the Russian armies in German-held territory. The Russians brought with them powerful weapons which the partisans could use against the Germans. Many of these partisans were incorporated into the ranks of the regular Soviet army. Many fell in battle. A large number of Jewish soldiers were highly decorated for their efforts against the Nazis and rose to positions of prominence in the Soviet army.

In a moving passage Shalom Cholawski, a Jewish fighter from the Nesvizh ghetto who fought in a partisan unit, conveys what it meant to be able to fight as soldiers against the Germans. He writes that when the Russian army finally appeared,

> We left the forest on July 12, 1944—a Jewish partisan unit named Zhukov [for the rising Russian general]. Our flag did not wave in the breeze though it fluttered in every heart. On a golden summer day between fields of ripening corn, we walked forward. The forest gradually fell back into the distance; I paused to look back. Near small woods and hills, clusters of Red Army men prepared for the crushing assault on the city of Baranovichi. From the edge of a wood came an elderly looking Russian officer, who, with a voice choked with joyful tears, cried out, "Yidden partisaner [Jewish partisan]!" He embraced us in true camaraderie.[32]

For Cholawski and his fighting comrades the greeting was tremendously important. It meant that the Jews were accepted by the Russian army as fighters against the Germans and resisters of the Holocaust, not only as its victims.

units of the Soviet army. It was important for the retreating Germans to maintain contact with each other and with Berlin. Several Jewish partisan groups focused sabotage efforts on increasingly vulnerable German communications lines, successfully hindering German withdrawals.

They occasionally attacked German convoys and succeeded in destroying a good deal of Germany military equipment. The partisan group of which Smolar (Yefim Stolerovitch) was a member killed one of the German commanders in the Minsk area, General Wilhelm Kube, by detonating a bomb planted in his house.

Holland

*In that hell they lived in, they have
maintained a human image.*
—Yitzhak Zuckerman,
A Surplus of Memory

In Holland, or the Netherlands, resistance to the Holocaust took on a different character than in other western European countries, largely because, unlike Denmark, whose Jewish population was a mere 8,000, in 1940 Holland included more than 140,000 Jews. Fewer than 15,000 were recent arrivals. Many Dutch Jews held influential and important positions in higher education, the law, commerce, and the arts.

Unlike France, where endemic anti-Semitism found a natural outlet during World War II, Holland prided itself on its liberal democratic traditions and its respect for the law. For most people in Holland, therefore, the defense of constitutionally guaranteed rights and, by extension, the Dutch Jews who also enjoyed their protection was tied to Dutch patriotism and Dutch morality. Many perceived threats to Dutch Jews as an attack on Dutch identity itself.

The lives of Holland's Jews suddenly were disrupted by the German invasion of 1940. The attack was swift and efficient. One citizen of Amsterdam recalls that

At seven in the evening of May 14, General Winkelman [head of the Dutch armed forces] came onto the radio and announced that the Germans had obliterated Rotterdam with bombs dropping from the air; that floods were spreading across sections of Holland through open dikes; that the Germans had threatened to bomb Utrecht and Amsterdam if we continued to resist. In order to spare further loss of life and property, the General explained, we were surrendering to the Germans.[33]

The Dutch royal family fled to London. The Germans took control of the Dutch government immediately upon the official surrender of May 15. The struggle had lasted only a few days. Hitler then appointed Arthur Seyss-Inquart, his longtime ally, *Reichskommissar* (supreme head of all affairs) of Holland, with full support of the SS and of the German police.

When the Germans first arrived, they assured the Jews of Holland that no harm would come to them. Two months later the Germans announced new restrictive policies toward Jews. They forced Jews out of government jobs and deprived them of their property. Jews no longer were permitted to own businesses in Holland. Ritual animal

Amsterdam, Holland, after Hitler's armies invaded in 1940. Shortly after the Germans conquered Holland, they began to impose restrictions on Holland's Jews.

slaughter was prohibited. Jews were expelled from clubs and organizations in which non-Jews participated. The Germans banned the publication of Jewish newspapers and ordered all Jews in the country to register with the authorities or face harsh punishment. In short, according to Louis de Jong, "From the autumn of 1940 to the summer of 1942 [the Jews] were subjected to a series of humiliating measures which drove them into social isolation and which undermined and destroyed their human dignity."[34]

Dutch Protest

Unlike many Poles, Ukrainians, and Latvians who willingly assisted the Germans in rounding up Jews, the majority of the people of Holland reacted immediately and negatively to what they considered illegal treatment of their fellow citizens. Although the German-controlled Dutch government itself did not protest, most leaders of the Protestant and Catholic churches in the country denounced the anti-Semitic measures.

Non-Jewish students staged public demonstrations at several Dutch universities. At the University of Leiden, for example, the head of the legal faculty, R. P. Cleveringa, publicly expressed his anger at the dismissal of one of the country's most celebrated legal scholars, Professor E. M. Meijers. Historian de Jong calls that speech one that "will always remain one of the finest manifestations of moral courage which have come from occupied Europe."[35] The Germans closed the universities at Leiden and Delft as punishment for the demonstrations.

Jewish resistance groups began to form in Amsterdam to protect the Jews of the capital from marching storm troopers who attacked individuals and damaged Jewish property. Young Jews meeting to discuss how best to protect themselves frequently were joined by non-Jewish workmen of the capital. The Germans responded by rounding up approximately 450 men on February 22 and 23, 1942. The detainees were forced into military lorries and ultimately sent to Mauthausen concentration camp. The Dutch learned eventually that all of the men deported in February 1942 were executed.

For three days the politically left-wing dockworkers in Amsterdam walked off the job to protest the violent treatment of their fellows. The Amsterdam dockworkers' strike demonstrating opposition to the deportation of the young Jews is unique in the history of the resistance to the Holocaust.

The Germans soon crushed the strike, however, and no more mass strikes or protests in Holland were carried out. With the German crackdown the Dutch realized that they were powerless to confront the German military forces stationed in their country.

In the spring of 1942 the Germans ordered all Dutch Jews to affix a yellow star on their outer clothing above their hearts. This action angered the Dutch. Miep Gies, a Christian, naturalized Dutch citizen who had been born in Austria but who lived in Amsterdam, describes the community's outrage at this latest German attack on Dutch Jews:

On the day that this order was to begin, many Dutch Christians, deeply rankled by the humiliation of our Jews, also wore yellow stars on their coats. Many wore yellow flowers, as emblems of solidarity, in their lapels or in their hair. Signs appeared in some shops asking Christians to show special respect for our Jewish neighbors, suggesting, for instance, that we lift our hats to them in a cheerful greeting—anything to show them that they were not alone.

Many Dutch did what they could to show their solidarity. This edict, somehow so much more enraging than all the others, was bringing our fierce Dutch anger to a boil. The yellow stars and yellow flowers those first few days were so common that our River Quarter was known as the Milky Way. The Jewish Quarter was laughingly called Hollywood. A surge of pride and solidarity swelled briefly until the Germans started cracking heads and making arrests. A threat was delivered to the population at large: anyone assisting Jews in any way would be sent to prison and possibly executed.[36]

This show of solidarity, though heartening, did not alter the course of events. In Holland as elsewhere, despite the protests of the Dutch population, the Germans were determined to exterminate the country's Jewish population.

In 1942 the German authorities began rounding up Dutch Jews and transporting them on public conveyances to assembly centers in Amsterdam itself. Then the Jews were taken to Westerbork, the local detention center. The Germans insisted that the Jews were merely to be "resettled" in the eastern part of Europe.

The people of Holland did not yet know about the death camps. They believed Allied propaganda that the Germans would soon

Children crawl through the barbed wire that the Germans used to close off Amsterdam's Jewish ghetto from the rest of the city.

be defeated. So they resigned themselves to the belief that for a period of time the Jews of Holland would live difficult lives in work camps making war supplies for the Germans and their Axis partners. The Jews of Holland did not organize against their deportation. Nor did the non-Jewish Dutch.

Once the roundups were underway the deportation trains left Westerbork detention camp every Tuesday. From 2000 to 3000 men, women, and children at a time were crammed into freight cars moving eastward to "resettlement areas." The Dutch people watched as the trains left. The Dutch Nazi Party, under the leadership of Hans Albin Rauter, assisted the Gestapo, or secret police, in punishing any Dutch who attempted to obstruct the deportation process. In the end, 75 percent of all Dutch Jews, some 105,000 people, were deported: Most of them died at Auschwitz and Sobibor concentration camps. Only 5 percent of Dutch Jews who were deported returned from the German camps after the war.

Jews Attempt to Hide

What happened to the Jews of Holland who did not disappear into the trains? A small

Jews arrive in Westerbork for transport to death camps. Jews cooperated with the relocation, refusing to believe in the rumors that they would be killed.

number of young people did manage to escape from Holland, mostly Zionists who had been involved in collective farming in the countryside and who hoped one day to go to Palestine. After some terrifying exploits, many were able to achieve their objective. A handful however, those who were particularly skillful at forging German documents, instead set up a printing shop at the Hotel Versigny in Paris.

This group, led by Kurt Reilinger, continued to provide false papers to fugitive Jews until 1944. On April 27, 1944, the Gestapo discovered the location of their printing shop, broke into their Paris office, and arrested the Dutch printers.

Over twenty thousand other Dutch Jews attempted to go underground (in Dutch, *onder te duiken*, to dive "under the dikes") within Holland itself. That is, they became *onderduikers*, those who lived underground. These people were assisted by Dutch men and women who were willing to risk their lives in order to save other human beings. They knew that they would share the fate of the Jews if they were caught. The early years of German occupation clearly demonstrated that they were not benign occupiers. But those people who assisted in hiding Dutch Jews did so because they refused to compromise their consciences by doing nothing.

Johannes Bogaard was one of these people. Bogaard was a farmer who lived not far from Amsterdam. When he learned that the deportations had begun, he went to the capital and located people who were willing to hide on his farm in order to avoid capture and deportation. His family supported him: Bogaard later said that "My father, with two of my brothers, one sister and my daughter to help had sixty-nine people on his farm; my other brother had thirteen; and I too,

Johannes Bogaard on his farm in Holland. Bogaard and his family worked together to hide Jewish children from the Nazis.

had thirteen permanent but there were always more."[37] A son was active in the Dutch underground and assisted in the rescue work.

During that terrible summer of 1942, several Jewish families marked for deportation learned about Bogaard's efforts and begged him to take their children. Why did Bogaard behave so bravely in secreting these Jewish children? "Can you imagine," he wrote years later, "what that meant to the parents, to give their children to someone they had never seen, whom they knew nothing about, not even his name? I had one family with seven

The Bogaard brothers hold hands with two of the Jewish children they hid from the Nazis during World War II.

children. Their grief was worse, much worse, than all the danger I ran."[38]

Thousands of people in Holland, laypeople and members of the clergy, acted as Johannes Bogaard did. They hid Jews in barns and in attics, in caves and in pits. Sometimes even neighbors did not know until after the war that Jews had been hidden for years on immediately adjoining property.

Part of the unique difficulty for the Dutch Jews and those who tried to hide them lay in Dutch geography. As Haim Avni points out: "The extreme density of the population and the lack of natural hiding places, drastically limited the possibility of evading the German authorities."[39] Moreover, there was

no adjacent neutral country to which they could escape in case of danger.

The price for aiding or harboring Jews was high. Bogaard's father and brother were arrested and died in concentration camps. His son died shortly after being released from a camp. But by their actions the Bogaard family saved some three hundred people. And about forty-five hundred hidden Jewish children all over Holland were alive when the war ended.

Otto Frank and His Family

The most well known of Dutch *onderduikers* are the members of the family of Otto Frank. On June 5, 1942, Edith and Otto

Frank and their two daughters, Margot Betti and Anneliese Marie, known as Anne, gathered up their essential belongings and hid in the upper floors of Frank's business, after Margot received special papers ordering her to report for forced labor service in Germany.

The Franks were originally from Frankfurt, Germany. They had long been part of the wealthy banking and business community of that city and Otto Frank had fought for Germany in World War I. He was decorated for his service and rose to the rank of lieutenant in the German army.

German persecution had since forced the Franks to escape to Holland. In Amsterdam Otto Frank set up a very successful import/export business called Travies and Company. In 1940 the German-controlled Dutch government forced Frank to register his business in the name of a Gentile partner. But he continued to run Travies and Company while making preparations to safeguard his family.

He prepared rooms on the upper floors of his business and laid stocks of dried provisions such as rice and beans. He also made arrangements with several trusted employees who willingly endangered their lives to protect the Franks. Three members of the van Pels family also went into hiding with the Franks.

Their hiding place, which the Franks called the Secret Annex, has become known throughout the world through "Kitty," the name Anne Frank gave to the diary she received on her thirteenth birthday, June 12, 1943, and which she kept for the two and half years of her concealment.

Though hiding from the Nazis with her family, Anne Frank still managed to express the longings and dreams of an adolescent girl. The inscription she wrote on this photo speaks of her wish to remain as she is pictured, so that she might someday have a chance to go to Hollywood. Anne died in Bergen-Belsen in 1945.

In the tiny rooms of the Secret Annex, Anne Frank grew into adolescence. She hung pictures of her favorite film stars—Ray Milland, Greta Garbo, and Ginger Rogers—on her wall. Present-day visitors to the Secret Annex, preserved as a memorial, can see them still.

Anne wrote daily in her diary, a small, reddish-colored clothbound book that became her intimate friend. The *Diary of a Young Girl* is the unself-conscious account of a young and talented child learning about the world and hoping for the best in people despite the constant danger which tormented her life.

The Franks and the van Pels were able to live in the annex through the efforts of Miep and Henk Gies and two other assistants who had worked for the Franks in the import business. They toiled at the risk of their lives to support the Jews hiding in the secret rooms. If their activities had been discovered, the Germans would have deported them along with the Franks and van Pels.

The Gieses were in contact with members of the Dutch underground through

"Be Brave!"

Anne Frank spent two years in hiding from the Germans in Amsterdam. The words of this brave young girl's diary are filled with human defiance and a burning will to live. The following extract, from *The Diary of a Young Girl*, is the entry for April 11, 1944

> Who has inflicted this upon us? Who has made us Jews different from all other people? Who has allowed us to suffer so terribly up till now? It is God that has made us as we are, but it will be God, too, who will raise us up again. If we bear all this suffering and if there are still Jews left, when it is over, then Jews, instead of being doomed, will be held up as an example.
>
> Who knows, it might even be our religion from which the world and all peoples learn good, and for that reason and that reason only do we have to suffer now. We can never become just Netherlanders, or just English, or representatives of any other county for that matter, we will always remain Jews, but we want to, too.
>
> Be brave! Let us remain aware of our task and not grumble, a solution will come. God has never deserted our people. Right through the ages there have been Jews, through the ages they have had to suffer, but it has made them strong too; the weak fall, but the strong will remain and never go under!
>
> During that night I really felt that I had died, I waited for the police, I was prepared, as the soldier is on the battlefield. I was eager to lay down my life for the country, but now, now I've been saved again, now my first wish after the war is that I may become Dutch! I love the Dutch, I love this country, I love the language and want to work here. And even if I have to write to the Queen myself, I will not give up until I have reached my goal.

whom they were able to obtain false ration cards for seven people, so that there would be adequate food for those in hiding. Miep Gies writes that when she used all her coupons the shopkeepers "pretended not to notice the large quantities of food she obtained on a regular basis. No words were exchanged but many silently participated in the attempt to hide the Jews in the Annex."[40] She writes that some shopkeepers put aside extra supplies for her. Others made special deliveries and tried in other ways to ease the burden she and her husband had decided to shoulder.

Unfortunately, the Franks and their companions were not among the fortunate few who survived the war. Someone, perhaps a disgruntled former employee, betrayed them on August 4, 1944, in an anonymous call to the offices of the German Security Services. The annex was raided by the SS, and the Franks and the van Pels were deported to concentration camps.

Edith Frank died in Auschwitz shortly after her deportation. Both Margot and Anne died of typhus in Bergen-Belsen in March 1945, four weeks before the camp was liberated. Neither did the van Pels survive the war.

Only Otto Frank returned to Amsterdam and the Gieses, who gave Anne's diary to him. They had retrieved it after the SS had flung it to the floor when they ransacked the Secret Annex during the roundup of its occupants.

Although Anne Frank died in Bergen-Belsen, the beauty and nobility of her young spirit has been immortalized. Her diary has been translated into all the world's languages, read by millions, and performed on the stage for audiences around the world.

The celebrity accorded the *Diary of a Young Girl* is not simply the response of a guilty world to the tragic death of a young girl. Rather, the book demonstrates the ability of the human spirit to resist oppression under the most severe circumstances. Anne resisted the Holocaust with all her might. Her love of life, her appreciation of nature, her hopes for her future and for those with whom she hid, fill the pages of her diary until the day she was captured. The *Diary* demonstrates how one young girl successfully resisted the efforts of the Nazis to dehumanize her.

Anne Frank also immortalized the bravery many Dutch people demonstrated toward their fellows. In the face of certain death if they were caught, many thousands of Dutch people dedicated themselves to resisting the Holocaust.

A higher percentage of Jews died in Holland than in any other country of western Europe. Living conditions in Holland were extremely brutal. The watchful eyes of the Germans were everywhere and they and their spies were extremely difficult to evade. The eighteen thousand Jewish survivors and those who protected them demonstrated an uncommon willingness and an uncommon valor to resist the brutality of the German occupation and the Holocaust.

You shall love the Lord your God with all your heart, with all your strength, with all your mind; and your neighbor as yourself.

—Deuteronomy 6:4-9

An extraordinary display of resistance to the Holocaust took place in France on the Plateau Vivarais-Lignon in the Department of Haute-Loire, in the south-central region of France. There in a tiny community called Le Chambon-sur-Lignon and a dozen surrounding villages, lives were saved during World War II.

Ironically, the cluster of villages lies near the town of Vichy. This is where the government of Marshal Henri-Philippe Pétain, which collaborated with the German occupation forces during World War II, established its headquarters.

Le Chambon is a remote village. It rests high on a volcanic plateau and the countryside is dotted with pastures and woods. Bitter, piercingly cold weather lasts for nine months and the ice that covers many of the roads forces people to stay indoors most of the time.

Tourist trade in the summer is the primary source of income for the people of Chambon. Many houses in and around the village are rented out to tourists. In addition, many villagers earn incomes from small farms radiating outward from the center of Chambon.

Its very isolation made the three-thousand-foot-high plateau region attractive to Huguenots, the French term for Protestants. Huguenots fled there in the sixteenth, seventeenth, and eighteenth centuries to escape religious persecution by intolerant Catholic rulers.

Protestants represent less than 1 percent of the French population. For many years they lived as a despised and threatened minority. Modern Huguenots are very familiar with the stories of their ancestors' persecution. Chambon historian Pierre Sauvage writes that "the memory of their past was the key to their survival."[41] They knew full well that over the centuries many French Protestants had paid with their lives trying to protect their religious beliefs.

In the 1940s many of the residents of Chambon and the surrounding villages were the direct descendants of the persecuted Protestants who once fled there for safety. Their continued impact in the region is demonstrated by the fact that there were close to nine thousand Protestants out of a total population of approximately twenty-four thousand people who lived on the Plateau Vivarais-Lignon.

In the tiny village of Chambon itself, twenty-five hundred Protestants lived side

The village of Le Chambon-sur-Lignon. The entire village of Le Chambon cooperated to save Jewish lives from the Nazis.

by side with approximately three hundred Catholic neighbors. The people in the region lived very modestly. They wore wooden shoes, they had no electricity, they read their Bibles, and they lived their faiths.

Pastor Trocmé

In 1934 André Pascal Trocmé became pastor of the village of Chambon. In 1938 he was joined by his friend and colleague Edouard Theis. Theis and Trocmé believed in a nonviolent response to violent confrontation. Both were inspired by and revered Jesus of Nazareth. As ethicist Philip Hallie writes:

Trocmé believed also that Jesus had demonstrated that love for mankind by

dying for us on the cross. And if these beliefs sounded too mysterious, he knew that Jesus had himself refused to do violence to mankind, refused to harm the enemies of his precious existence as a human being. In short, Jesus was for Trocmé the embodiment of forgiveness of sins, and staying close to Jesus meant always being ready to forgive your enemies instead of torturing and killing them.[42]

These deeply religious men served in Chambon at a time when their country faced mounting internal and external difficulties. The worldwide depression had taken a terrible financial toll of people at the same time

Le Chambon-sur-Lignon   55

that the threat of war with Germany widened deep conflicts among the various political parties in France. As the 1930s drew to a close the very continuation of the Third French Republic was in jeopardy.

There were many Frenchmen who ardently supported the democratic and liberal traditions of the French republic. At the same time many others, royalists, reactionaries, and ultranationalists, were prepared to overthrow republican institutions and collaborate with the rising fascist forces in Europe.

These divisions within French political life made it impossible for the country to mount an effective defense when Germany attacked France on May 10, 1940. The highly regarded French army surrendered within a matter of weeks. On June 14 German troops entered Paris. On June 22 Marshal Pétain signed an armistice with the Germans. Germany took control over the northern part of France.

Administratively the southern part of the country remained under the control of Pétain and his colleagues, who established their government in Vichy. Until November 11, 1942, when Germany took over all of France, Vichy France remained nominally the "free zone" of the country.

Even before France signed an armistice with Nazi Germany, Jewish refugees from Germany and central Europe started arriving in the Plateau Vivarais-Lignon in the "free zone." In Chambon the one o'clock train brought the occasional foreign travelers who sometimes made their way first to the Protestant parsonage to seek advice.

Now native French Jews began to arrive. They knew about Chambon from past vacations in the region. They started coming south out of fear of what German occupation of the north would mean to themselves and their families. They rented apartments and rooms from the people in Chambon and the surrounding villages. Writer Albert Camus and many other famous Frenchmen eventually rented living space in the region. These refugees knew of the opposition of the people of the region to violence and religious discrimination.

On Sunday, June 22, 1940, the day of the signing by Pétain of the armistice with Germany, the pastors of the Chambon church voiced their concerns for the future. They reminded their parishioners that

> The duty of Christians is to resist the violence that will be brought to bear on their consciences through the weapons of

A Frenchman weeps as German troops march into Paris in June 1940. As they had done in many other countries they occupied, the Germans imposed heavy anti-Semitic sanctions.

Hiding the Jews

Pastor Trocmé would not conceal from the authorities his and his parish's attitude toward the anti-Semitic policies of the Vichy government. He took advantage of the official visit of Minister Laminard to Le Chambon to state his opinion through the vehicle of a letter the students of the school gave Mr. Laminard. Philip Hallie, in *Lest Innocent Blood Be Shed*, presents the letter in full.

> We have learned of the frightening scenes which took place three weeks ago in Paris, where the French police, on orders of the occupying powers, arrested in their homes all the Jewish families in Paris to hold them in the Vel D'Hiv. The fathers were torn from their families and sent to Germany. The children torn from their mothers, who underwent the same fate as their husbands. Knowing by experience that the decrees of the occupying powers are, with brief delay imposed on Unoccupied France, where they are presented as the spontaneous decisions of the head of the French government..., we are afraid that the measures of deportation of the Jews will soon be applied in the Southern Zone.

> We feel obliged to tell you that there are among us a certain number of Jews. But, we make no distinction between Jews and non-Jews. It is contrary to the Gospel teaching.

> If our comrades, whose only fault is to be born in another religion, received the order to let themselves be deported, or even examined, they would disobey the orders received, and would try to hide them as best we could.

the spirit. We will resist whenever our adversaries will demand of us obedience contrary to the orders of the Gospel. We will do so without fear but also without pride and without hate.[43]

Roundup of French Jews

This inspired appeal to passive resistance came none too soon. The armistice spelled the doom for one-third of the Jews of France. Almost immediately harsh anti-Semitic laws were enacted. France provided Hitler with more assistance to find and deport its Jewish population than any other country in western Europe. A surprisingly large number of French police willingly followed the orders of their German conquerors.

Marshal Pétain showed his own support for Hitler and for fascism by signing even more severe anti-Semitic legislation than his German masters expected of him. The *Milice*, those French police who acted on behalf of the Vichy government (not German soldiers), brutally carried out the capture and deportation of Jews in France.

Historian Milton Meltzer spells out what happened in France under Pétain and his fascist allies. He writes that the government of Pétain had two options:

Marshal Philippe Pétain imposed even harsher anti-Semitic sanctions than the Nazi invaders.

To join the Germans in persecuting the Jews or to protect the Jews and resist their deportation. The choice of the Vichy government was soon clear. Within months of the surrender to the Germans in 1940 it adopted racist laws that were in some ways harsher than Germany's.[44]

Anti-Semitic measures became more and more violent. At first Jews were forced out of public jobs. Then many people were compelled to turn over their businesses to the government. Some were openly attacked on the streets of Paris. Then men, women, and children were pulled off the streets and placed in detention camps.

The people of Chambon read about these events and heard first-person accounts from some of the refugees. While Trocmé advocated nonviolence, he and his parishioners could not remain passive in the face of the persecution of their fellow Frenchmen, the Jews. And so the people of the region, singly and collectively, almost spontaneously, began taking part in acts of passive resistance.

In the words of Trocmé's daughter, Nelly Trocmé Hewett, Trocmé, Theis, the people of Chambon and in the surrounding parishes simply "tried to implement what they said they believed in"[45] as the violence came close to their own homes.

The protection of innocent lives was a central precept of their religious faith. They believed that "You shall love your neighbor as yourself,"[46] even if it meant risking your own life to do so. When an old woman of Chambon was asked recently why she helped during the war, she answered simply, "The Bible says to feed the hungry."[47]

During the dark years of World War II in Chambon, the pastors' faith and that of the rural people who were their flock were put to the test. Their resistance to the Holocaust demonstrated that "The human spirit can rise to the highest challenges when those challenges come their way."[48]

The Quakers

André Trocmé went to Marseilles to the headquarters of the American Friends Service

Committee to volunteer to work in a French detention camp. He spoke with Bruns Chambers, who ran the office in the city.

Chambers told Trocmé that he and his parishioners would be of far more service working outside the camps. He asked if they could offer shelter for children if they could be rescued from the camps and from hiding places throughout the country. Thousands of young French Jews, members of various underground resistance movements, worked to rescue Jewish children.

Organizations such as the Jewish Fighting Organization, the Armée Juive (the Jewish Army), L'Union des Juifs pour la Resistance, and in particular Jewish units of the Scouts dedicated themselves to saving Jewish children. Sometimes they convinced Jewish parents in detention camps to relinquish their children to them. Jewish resistance fighters often were able to smuggle children out of their homes, orphanages, and internment camps and place them in hiding with families. Many of the children found shelter within facilities established by the Quakers and by the Catholic Church that, on the local level, offered considerable help to refugees.

Trocmé agreed to participate in these rescues and knew his parishioners would also. The people wished to help, the tourist homes made placement possible, and the pastors of the villages had agreed that this was the best way in which they could assist in the rescue efforts. The French Jewish underground, the Quakers, and other organizations knew now that they could place children in Chambon and in the surrounding villages.

Historian Milton Meltzer points out that "American organizations such as the Quakers, the Unitarians and the YWCA fought hard with the Vichy regime to win authorization to take Jewish children out of the detention camps."[49] Although their agitation did not stop the deportations, it did unveil the cloak of secrecy behind which Pétain had tried to hide his collaboration with the Germans. Historian David Wyman suggests that "although the protests failed to stop the evacuations, they may have contributed to the fact that the Nazis never undertook another large-scale removal of France's native-born Jews."[50]

The rescuers' major challenges came in the summer of 1942, when the Germans began the deportation of French Jews east to concentration camps. The Germans, numbering perhaps twenty-five hundred men, but aided by thirty-five thousand Frenchmen, undertook a huge roundup of

Some of the Jewish children sheltered at Le Chambon. Under the guidance of the town's two influential pastors, all of its citizens made it their duty to shelter Jewish children.

The Deportation

The largest of the deportations of Jews from France took place during July and August 1942. The assistance of the French police made the roundups possible, as the German force in Paris was relatively small. It was the French who were able to discover the hiding places of many Jews, particularly of children who had been placed by their parents in the care of friends, relatives, and the Catholic Church. The news of these events deepened the Trocmés' determination to continue their work of protecting those who sought their assistance. They learned from others about the horrifying events of those summer days. The following information is taken from *The Abandonment of the Jews: America and the Holocaust* by David S. Wyman. One report comes from some French citizens who watched the trains leaving. The second comes from Donald Lowrie, an American YMCA relief worker who had been working with the refugees in Paris just before the massive deportations.

"We were at the camp des Milles the day the last train left," reported two French citizens. "The spectacle was indescribably painful to behold. All the internees had been lined up with their pitifully battered valises tied together with bits of string. Most of them were in rags, pale, thin, worn out with the strain. . . . Many of them were quietly weeping. . . . Their faces showed only hopeless despair."

Donald Lowrie, the YMCA worker, wrote to his headquarters in New York City. "The actual deportation was as bad as could be imagined; men and women pushed like cattle into box-cars, thirty to a car, whose only furniture was a bit of straw on the floor, one iron pail for all toilet purposes and a police guard. The journey, we were told, would take a fortnight or eighteen days.

All of us were curtly refused permission to accompany the trains or even to organize a service of hot drinks and refreshments at the frontier where they passed into German occupied territory."

French Jews in Paris. Between July 6 and 17 alone, twenty-eight thousand Jews were captured. Ultimately ninety thousand French Jews, nearly a third of the entire Jewish population of France, were rounded up.

At first these people were placed in detention camps. Then they were placed on trains and shipped off to concentration camps where they were murdered by the Germans with the assistance of the French authorities.

During the massive July 1942 raid, single people immediately were placed in the Drancy concentration camp, just three miles northeast of Paris. Families with children were crowded into the Veldrome D'Hiver, a sports arena in Paris where they suffered for days without food, water, or toilet facilities. Then they, too, were sent to Drancy, the major concentration camp in France. From there they were shipped to Auschwitz. The group included 4,051 children. None survived the war.

The people of the Chambon region saw the dire importance of their rescue efforts. The trickle of humanity who had found their way to Chambon became a veritable flood in the second half of the war. The Vichy authorities were aware of the resistance activities. George Lamirand, the Vichy minister for youth, came to Chambon in the summer of 1942. He wanted to make sure the village would turn over any Jewish refugees if it was required to do so.

The students of the local school presented to the minister a letter that had been written by Pastors Trocmé and Theis. The letter reflected the opposition of the people of Chambon to the Vichy actions against the Jews of Paris. In part the letter stated: "We have learned of the frightening scenes which took place three weeks ago in Paris. . . . We feel obliged to tell you that there are among us a certain number of Jews. But, we make no distinction between Jews and non-Jews. It is contrary to the Gospel teachings."[51]

Jews are unloaded from trucks at a railway station to be transported to Drancy concentration camp. From Drancy, Jews were shipped to Auschwitz.

Foiled Roundup of Jews

Later in the year, Vichy authorities came to Le Chambon to conduct a roundup of Jews. Trocmé told the Germans that he did not recognize the difference between Jews and Christians. On that occasion the Vichy officials stayed for three weeks, hoping to capture refugees. In the end the Nazis left with their buses empty. From the wooded countryside around Chambon small groups of children and adults began to reemerge to return to their places of shelter.

The Germans were aware of the rescue movement of the area since the Chambonnais' activities were relatively open. At one point the Vichy police arrested Trocmé, Theis, and a third man, the schoolmaster Roger Darcissac. The entire village assembled as the three men were led away. They were taken to an internment camp where they continued to preach their religious beliefs and from which, after a short time, they were released. Their experience in custody, while alarming, did not stop the rescue efforts of the three men, their wives, or the community.

Chambon thus became a place of refuge for people, mostly children who had been removed from southern internment camps. Few other French villages were willing to expose themselves to such extreme dangers and very few had the readily available rooming facilities to do so.

A Community Effort

The Quakers were among several organizations which helped fund, feed, and clothe children as the Plateau Vivarais-Lignon continued its rescue work until the end of the war. The Quakers left France entirely when the Germans occupied Vichy France in 1942. But their runners continued to send money from Switzerland until the very end of the war to support the rescue efforts in the villages. The boardinghouses and the private homes remained open to the children the area had undertaken to protect. No one seeking shelter was turned away.

As part of this sheltering effort, Pastor Trocmé, his Italian-born wife, Magda, and their four children shared their own modest home with refugees who needed a place to stay. There was "Monsieur Colin" the cabinetmaker whose real name was Kohn and the cook "Madame Berthe," (Madame Grunhut) as well as two French students who were attending school in Chambon. Their guests varied in number. When the gendarmes paid visits to the

(From left) André Trocmé, Roger Darcissac, and Edouard Theis pose for the camera after their release from an internment camp. The three were arrested on February 13, 1943.

A New Name

Efforts were made to "aryanize" many of the children in hiding so that even if Germans discovered them, their identity would go undetected. In *Rescue*, by Milton Meltzer, one woman who worked with the children tells the following story.

One day I was so upset about a little boy who had already changed his name once before, in order to make it sound less Polish-Jewish and more French-Jewish, and now had to change it again, to make it sound more French-Christian. To comfort me, he said, "Don't worry, I'm getting used to new names." Then all of a sudden he mused, "Maybe nobody remembers my real name."

Trocmés, M. Colin and Mme. Berthe disappeared into the recesses of the parsonage.

Other homes and farms in the area accepted children to live over the course of the war. Some children came and went. Some stayed for the duration of the war. Throughout the course of the occupation, regardless of the danger, no child in shelter in Chambon was lost; no traitor ever betrayed the secrets of the villages.

Pastors Trocmé and Theis worked side by side, guided by their strong spiritual beliefs. In addition to his work in the church, Edouard Theis also served as director of the Cévenole School in the village. Trocmé had founded the school in 1938 as the village's first secondary school. It was a most unusual establishment, inspired by a belief in the need for people all over the world to cooperate with one another and other nonviolent, coeducational, and Protestant principles. At that time the school had eighteen students.

During the war the Cévenole School grew dramatically in size. Classes were held in locations all over the village, and even in the kitchens and back rooms of homes. The local carpenter built benches and chairs for improvised classrooms needed to provide for the expanded student body of over three hundred students, thirty teachers, and fifteen heads of school who participated in this unique educational experience.

In spite of the violence around them, the teachers at the school continued to tell their students of the goal of pursuing pacifism and internationalism. However, at the same time Trocmé and Theis preached to the students "resistance against the hatred, betrayal, and naked destruction that Nazi Germany stood for." The faculty insisted in those terrible times, "when some nations were trying to appease Hitler, that a nation, like an individual, must do all it can to resist evil."[52]

Roger Darcissac, the director of the local public school in the village, was among the many people who contributed to the rescue efforts of the area. Darcissac's hobby was photography. He used his skills to counterfeit "official" documents for the ever-changing roster of students in his own school. Oscar Rosowsky assisted in the production of such papers. Oscar was an eighteen-year-old Jew who found shelter in Chambon after living in Marseilles, where he had worked for a printer. His extraordinary printing skills enabled him to produce many of the papers required by the people living on the Plateau. Oscar lived with the

Hertier family. When the Germans came to inspect the area, Oscar placed his documents and printing materials in empty beehives on the Hertier farm.

In addition to its role as a place for obtaining documents and providing shelter and schooling for refugees, the area also became something of an underground railroad depot. A group of local women formed an organization called the Cimade. The Cimade took small groups of people from Chambon to the Swiss border two hours away by train. One by one the refugees, mostly children, quietly crossed over into Switzerland when the German border guards could be evaded. The Cimade received assistance from the Scouts, who were particularly active in the border areas, Switzerland, and Spain, where the smuggling of Jewish children was possible.

Near the village various resistance fighters called the Maquis found shelter in the woods, undertaking acts of sabotage against the German occupying forces. They used violence in order to overthrow the Germans and they included an exceptionally large number of French Jews. In fact, it is estimated that while the Jewish population of

Members of the Maquis demonstrate how they placed dynamite demolition charges under a railroad trestle to disrupt rail traffic and delay Nazi supplies.

France numbered less than 1 percent of the population, the resistance movement was approximately 20 percent Jewish.

A Jewish fighter from Marseilles led one of these groups and helped to insure that no harm came to the communes on the Plateau. Perhaps it was he who passed the word to Trocmé and Theis that they were again to be arrested. Trocmé went into hiding for nine months until the Allies liberated France in 1944. Theis instead spent the remainder of the war working with the Cimade, which continued its underground railroad to Switzerland.

When the State of Israel was founded in 1948, its leaders wished to pay tribute to those people who had risked their lives to save Jews during the Holocaust. They established an organization, Yad Vashem, to examine the credentials of those people they thought worthy of being included in that small but honored group. André and Magda Trocmé, and Edouard Theis and his wife Mildred, were among those individuals whose names were included for consideration. The Israeli committee concluded that they had saved Jewish lives at the peril of their own and they received the Medal of Righteousness from grateful survivors of the Holocaust.

Upon further consideration, however, the Israeli committee decided that it was obligated to accord still greater recognition to all those who had been involved in what happened on the Plateau Vivarais-Lignon during the war. They understood that the World War II rescue efforts were largely spontaneous acts undertaken by the people of the area as a simple human response to the needs of people who required help. In 1990 the entire village and the surrounding communes were honored for their efforts during the war.

Denmark Saves Its Jews

It was a night of watching by the Lord, to bring them out of the land of Egypt; so this same night is a night of watching kept to the Lord by all the people of Israel throughout their generations.
—Exodus 12:42

German soldiers invaded Denmark on April 9, 1940. Within hours, the Danish army surrendered. The tiny Danish army was no match for the mighty Wehrmacht. Unlike other contemporary European rulers, however, Christian X, the seventy-year-old king of Denmark, did not flee to exile in London. He and his government remained in Denmark. Their presence in Copenhagen served as a symbol of Danish integrity because the king and his government were willing to share in the hardships associated with the occupation.

Also, unlike the situation elsewhere in Europe, the lives of Danish Jews were not jeopardized, at least not at first, by the presence of the German army. King Christian was aware of the terrible hardships suffered by Jews in Germany since the rise of Adolf Hitler in 1933. Christian made it a condition of his surrender that the Jews of Denmark would be treated no differently than anyone else. Danish Jews, he notified Hitler, were completely integrated into Danish society.

They were covered by all Danish laws and the government intended to enforce those laws.

In 1940 approximately eight thousand Jews lived in Denmark, the vast majority in

Danish youngsters are shown looking on in curiosity as invading German soldiers check and clean their rifles after entering Denmark.

Copenhagen, the Danish capital. Because their numbers were so small, the Danish Jews did not play a large role in Hitler's plans. So he decided he would not disrupt the good relations he enjoyed with the otherwise cooperative Danish government by moving against the Jews in 1940.

For Hitler, Denmark was his *Musterprotektorat*, or model protectorate. He regarded the Danes as fellow Aryans; that is, people who were related closely to the pure Germans by blood. For a few years the Danes maintained relatively good relations with the German occupying forces. In fact they supplied the German army with foodstuffs and thereby helped insure that their own rations would not be cut dramatically as had happened in other occupied countries.

The Jews of Denmark went about their lives quietly in the early years of the war. They were grateful for the protective position assumed by the Danish government. Jewish community leaders did not develop a strategy of self-defense, confident that the institutions of their own government would protect them as they would the rest of the Danish population.

An unsettling act of vandalism in 1942 led to what the Jews of Denmark hoped would be a consistent pattern of response on the part of the Danish government. Historian Harold Flender relates the following events:

Late in 1942 there was an attempt to set fire to the Copenhagen Synagogue. The action was prevented by Danish police. The only damage the Germans did was to paint a swastika on the Synagogue walls. To stop further attempts, the Danish police formed a special auxiliary police unit, composed of Danish Jews armed with clubs and guns who were

King of Denmark, Christian X refused to flee his country as the Nazis invaded. He wanted to show a sign of unity and support for his fellow citizens.

assigned to guard the Synagogue. The Danish police also set up an electric warning system with direct connections between the Synagogue and police headquarters.[53]

Germans Tighten Control

By 1943, however, there was reason to believe that Germany would soon end its relatively benign policies toward Denmark and Danish Jews. By then the tide of war had turned against Germany. Russian military might threatened the Wehrmacht in the east. Allied landings in North Africa threatened Germany's hold on the southern coast of Europe. With the war increasingly beyond his control Hitler determined to complete his second goal, annihilating the Jews of Europe.

So early in 1943 German thinking about the Danish situation began to change. Internal freedoms would be curtailed and the Jews would be eliminated. This change coincided with an increase in Danish resistance activity. Many Danes had grown increasingly uncomfortable with their role as food suppliers to the German army, particularly when their own food rations began to decrease.

The Danes were aware of German atrocities elsewhere in Europe. Acts of sabotage increased. In February thirty-four attacks were made on factories, railways, and other facilities. Small bombs strategically secreted in such places disrupted production of war material and foodstuffs and delayed the shipment of supplies to German field armies.

In April 1943, as the Warsaw ghetto uprising raged in Poland, the number of attacks on German installations rose to seventy-eight. As the Germans in Denmark increased their pressure against the Jews, the resistance movement seemed to gain momentum. Throughout this season of increasing tension King Christian assured his people that they had the continued support of the royal family.

The Germans dismissed the Danish cabinet. Berlin also decided that Cecil von Renthe-Fink, the civilian representative to Denmark from the German government, had been too lenient in his treatment of the Danes. Karl Werner Best replaced Renthe-Fink.

This was an ominous change. Best was a former administrative chief of the Gestapo who was eager to put himself into the good graces of Hitler. He wanted to show his support for the German Reich by destroying the Danish resistance movement and by removing the Jews of Denmark. Nevertheless, despite Best's efforts, the number of acts of sabotage against the Germans continued to increase. At the end of August the Germans finally declared martial law in Denmark in order to quell the increasing unrest. German troops appeared outside all government buildings in the country.

In response to the German takeover of the civilian government, the Danish navy made efforts to escape German control. Rear Admiral Vedel ran up a flag signal to the fleet captains: "Scuttle or escape to Sweden." Within moments of receiving the signal, the Danish navy ceased to exist. Part of the fleet escaped to Sweden, where it put itself under the protection of the Swedish government. Those Danish captains who were unable to escape scuttled their ships rather than surrender them to the German navy.

The Plan to Capture Jews

The Germans struggled to gain control over the Danish Jews by raiding the offices of the Jewish community center. The major item stolen was a list of the names and addresses of all the Jews who lived in the county, both native-born and recent immigrants. At the same time Georg Ferdinand Duckwitz, the officer at the German embassy in Copenhagen who was responsible for all shipping matters, received ominous orders. He was told to prepare a number of large cargo ships on which all captured Jews could be placed for transport to concentration camps.

At this point Best sent Hitler what turned out to be a premature telegram, telling him that Denmark would soon be free of Jews. Despite the fact that he was a German officer, Duckwitz did not agree with the policy of deporting the Jews of Denmark to concentration camps. So he informed a friend, Hans Hedtoft, an influential Dane who headed the Social Democratic Party, about Best's plans. Hedtoft in turn gave the information to H. C. Hansen, a Danish government official, who called into his office his longtime acquaintance, the head of the Jewish community in Copenhagen, C. B. Henriques.

Hansen told the internationally known attorney that the list containing the names of all Jews living in Denmark now was in the hands of the Gestapo. He strongly urged Henriques to convey this frightening information to the heads of the Jewish community and to warn them that a roundup of Jews was imminent.

Until this point the Jewish community leaders had tried to keep quiet about the theft from the community center in order not to alarm people. And though Henriques himself was reluctant to believe that the lives of Jews of Denmark were in any danger, he decided to take Hansen's advice to make public all that he knew. He paid a visit to Marcus Melchior, the chief rabbi in Copenhagen, to apprise him of what Hansen considered to be an imminent raid on the community.

Rabbi Melchior Warns the Community

Rabbi Melchior listened carefully as Henriques told him about the plans of the Gestapo. The Germans had ordered two large cargo ships to be available for the Gestapo to fill with Jews. The Germans intended to begin the roundup of the Jews of Denmark at 10 o'clock on the night of Friday, October 1, 1943, no doubt calculated to coincide with the evening of the Jewish New Year, Rosh Hashanna, when most

Jews would be either in the synagogue or in their homes, thus easy to capture. Melchior had two days in which to act.

On the morning of September 29, 1943, when the Jewish congregation assembled for religious services, the rabbi appeared before the people in unusual attire. Melchior was not wearing his sacramental robes. Instead he had on street clothing, including his black homburg hat, as if he was preparing to take a trip. He told the congregation what he had learned:

> There will be no service this morning. Instead, I have very important news to tell you. Last night I received word that tomorrow the Germans plan to raid all

Rabbi Marcus Melchior and his son in 1963. Before a planned roundup of Jews in his community, Melchior warned his congregation to seek hiding places.

Jewish homes throughout Copenhagen to arrest all the Danish Jews for shipment to concentration camps. We must take action immediately. You must leave the synagogue now and contact all relatives, friends and neighbors you know who are Jewish and tell them what I have told you. You must tell them to pass the word on to everyone they know is Jewish. You must also speak to all your Christian friends and tell them to warn the Jews. You must do this immediately, within the next few minutes, so that two or three hours from now everyone will know what is happening. By nightfall tonight, we must all be hiding.[54]

The congregation dispersed. The people returned to their homes and did as Rabbi Melchior advised. Fortunately for

them, the Germans did not cut the telephone lines in Copenhagen until the day of the planned *Aktion* so the Jews of the city were able to warn everyone they knew of the terrible danger facing the community. Jews, those Jews married to Christians, and recent immigrants received the warning many times from many different people. Often the warning came from members of the Danish resistance who had also been warned and who went into action.

Aktion Begins

On October 1, 1943, as planned, German forces began their *Aktion* against the Jews of Denmark. They cut the telephone lines of the city and arrived at the doors of Jewish homes. But the Jews had disappeared. Of the 8,000 Jews of the country the Germans rounded up only about 450, mostly old and

The Danish Underground

The Danish underground became increasingly active as the German government stepped up its campaign against the Jews. In 1965, Kai Johansen, an active member of the resistance during the German occupation, wrote an article describing what happened. The article is quoted in Elliott Arnold's, *A Night of Watching.*

> The action of the Danish Jews had a totally different effect to what the Nazis had foreseen. Up until then the various parts of the Resistance Movement—the military intelligence, parachutists, arms groups, saboteurs and the illegal press—had each worked by themselves without any real coordination. On those October nights along

the Danish coast and in the organization of transports to the ports and from there to Sweden—all this created a certain amount of coordination.

> This action against the Danish Jews was a decisive factor in the awakening of the majority of the Danish people to the realization of what they might expect if the Nazis won the war.

> The organized resistance period began. Random actions were replaced by coordination and systemization.

> From the autumn of 1943 Denmark was, if not formally, then nevertheless in reality, in the ranks of the Allied nations.

infirm individuals living in institutions whom the Danes had overlooked.

If there were any doubts about German intentions, the treatment accorded these unfortunate people made Danes realize how brutal the German occupiers could become. Erling Foss, a Danish writer, describes one awful scene:

> The old age-home next to the synagogue in Krystalgade was surrounded by 150 men, and all the inmates, aged from sixty to ninety, were taken away. The Germans behaved here with incredible brutality. They burst into the rooms of an old lady who was paralyzed and had been bed ridden for eleven years, and since she could not get up they bound her with leather straps and dragged her to the synagogue, where all the old people were assembled. Here they were cross-examined as to their acquaintance with this or that saboteur, and since it was only natural that they did not know any, they were beaten and kicked. From the synagogue, as from all the rooms, the Germans stole any valuables they could lay their hands on; and the German police troops relieved themselves in the synagogue.[55]

When the captives left Denmark, a crowd of Danes gathered to watch these wretched people go up the gangplank of one of the German cargo ships. A total of 472 people were captured during German raids over the next several days. Their Danish well-wishers gathered on the dock near the cargo ship and began to sing the Dan-ish national anthem to the unfortunate captives as they disappeared into the hold of the ship.

Where were the Jews? The people of Denmark had hidden them. Jews found hiding places in the homes of friends, religious institutions, hospitals, and churches. They disappeared into farms and barns and into the woods. Some went into hiding in Bispebjerg Hospital in Copenhagen where they were dispersed in many wards under Christian-sounding names. Rabbi Melchior and his own family took a train to the coastal home of a Lutheran pastor and long-time friend. The pastor hid the family for eight days until it was their turn to be smuggled into Sweden.

The Jews' sacred objects also disappeared. The pastors of the local churches rescued Torah scrolls and other objects from the synagogue and hid them for the duration of the war. Some were kept in the Royal Library, some in the Town Hall. The Germans had been foiled temporarily.

The religious institutions of Denmark played a major role in the protection of Jews, as exemplified by this nun escorting three Jewish girls across the German border to Denmark.

This extraordinary and unique act of human courage could not have taken place if the people of Denmark had not acted immediately and in unison to resist the danger facing the Jews of the country. "People from all walks of life reacted with conscience and a sense of personal responsibility," writes historian Harold Flender. "Thanks to the spontaneous willingness and cooperation of Jews and non-Jews, Rabbi Melchior's wish that within a matter of hours every Jew in Denmark would know of the danger facing him largely was fulfilled. Word was gotten to almost everyone directly concerned except the Germans."[56]

But the Jews of Denmark could not be hidden indefinitely. Permanent arrangements had to be made to secure the safety of eight thousand people. Fortunately, Danish officials already had been in contact with their counterparts in neutral Sweden. The Swedish people were dissatisfied with their government's assistance to Germany during the war, and the government was persuaded to demonstrate its high moral principles by agreeing to protect the Jews of Denmark if they could reach Sweden.

Historian Harold Flender relates a story that the Swedish nuclear scientist Niels Bohr, himself half-Jewish, played a role in finding a safe haven for the Jews of Denmark. Apparently Albert Einstein wanted Bohr to come to America to work with him on the development of the atomic bomb. But Bohr refused to leave Sweden. Flender writes that

Danish refugees arrive in Sweden after escaping from Denmark in small boats. The Swedes agreed to accept the Danish Jews if they could find a way to get to their country.

Bohr told the Swedish foreign office that he would not leave until the foreign minister promised to find refuge for all Danish Jews able to reach Sweden. King Gustav said that he was sympathetic to the problem and would give it careful consideration. The next day Bohr received word from King Gustav that Sweden would accept all the Jews of Denmark. Bohr still refused to go. He wanted it announced in the front pages of Sweden's leading newspaper and broadcast over radio to Denmark. After several days both announcements were made and Bohr left Sweden for the United States." [57]

From Kronborg Castle in the town of Elsinore on the Danish coast one can see Sweden across the water. Historian Elliott Arnold writes that "in the basement [of the castle] according to legend, lived Holger Danske, Holger the Dane, the protector of Denmark who awakened and went forth only in time of danger. Holger Danske was afoot again, it was said, embodied in one of the resistance groups which used his name." [58] The distance between Elsinore and Treleborg in Sweden is less than three miles across the narrows. It would be the longest sea journey, psychologically, in the lives of the Jewish fugitives who made the crossing.

Evacuation to Sweden

The Danish resistance made preparations to transport the Jews. With the assistance of the Danish police, the resistance fighters, many of them scarcely out of their teens, made arrangements to have Jews transported from their various hiding places to villages along the Danish coast. Some of the Jews, especially those who had fled into the forests, proved difficult to find, so Danish doctors and nurses from Bispebjerg Hospital went into the woods to locate the fugitives.

Over a period of eight days nearly all the Jews in hiding were transported safely to the coastal towns. Danish taxi drivers provided transportation for those who did not have money to make the trip by train. Members of the medical staff who had hidden Jews in hospital wards found transportation, sometimes in ambulances, in order to get their "patients" to the coast. Physicians gave sedatives to many of the children so that they would not cry out in fear and alert German guards.

Danish sea captains agreed to carry the dangerous human cargo to Sweden. At first some tried to charge exorbitant prices in exchange for risking their ships and their lives in the rescue effort. After all, mines in the Danish coastal waters could threaten their ships and German water patrols might question their activities. The Danish resistance fighters were not defeated by this attempt to take advantage of the perilous position of the Jews. As it worked out those Jews with extra money helped pay the way for those who were without funds. Danish citizens helped raise the remainder to cover the costs associated with the escape of the Jews from Denmark. Some Danish captains refused to accept any money from the refugees.

Lutheran pastors all over the country lent their assistance to the rescue. They hid Jews in their buildings, helped to raise money, and spoke out openly in support of the resistance movement. Pastor Ivar Lange of Frederiksberg Church was typical of the Danish clergy. On October 3, 1943, he read to his congregation the protest against German anti-Semitism written by the Danish Lutheran bishops. Then he added his own words:

"Like Herrings in a Barrel"

The scenes on the Danish coast of the rescue of the Jews were filled with tension and danger. One Jewish woman reported after the war what it had been like on the cold October night during which she was rescued. The quotation is taken from Milton Meltzer's *Rescue: The Story of How Gentiles Saved Jews in the Holocaust.*

A man came and gave the signal to start. We were taken by taxi to the beach near a little fishing harbor. Each of the four passengers and the organizer were then hidden under a bush by the shore. The plan was that at a certain time we were to crawl along the beach to the harbor, where there was a watchtower manned by Germans. We lay a whole day waiting for darkness. Up on the road we could hear cars drive by and we shiv-ered with fright. Once a truck stopped right opposite our hiding place, but luckily it contained underground fighters who comforted us with the news that there were armed resistance fighters in the nearby ditches. As far as we knew, the Germans in the watchtower had been bribed to turn a blind eye. At seven o'clock in the evening a strange sight revealed itself. From the bushes along the beach human forms crawled out on their stomachs. We discovered that these were other passengers of whose presence we had been completely unaware. After a while we reached the fishing boat without mishap and were herded into the hold, like herrings in a barrel. As there was not enough space down below, a few passengers were wrapped in fishing nets and in sacks on the deck.

Danish Jews set sail for Sweden to escape the Nazis.

Politics must not be discussed here, because it is punishable. In spite of this I tell you that I would rather die with the Jews than live with the Nazis."[59]

When they arrived safely in Sweden, the Danish Jews received a warm reception from well-wishers. People waited for them with warm clothing, food, and offers of money, shelter, and employment until the end of the war.

The Danish resistance to the German attempt to murder Jewish citizens did not end with their transportation to Sweden.

The Danish people took care of the property and possessions of the Jews while they were gone. They watered their plants, cared for their pets, and made certain that no one vandalized their property.

Danes Look Out for Jews

Neither did the Danish government and King Christian forget about the more than four hundred Jews who were taken to Theresienstadt concentration camp. Christian informed the German government that he took a special interest in the welfare of his people and insisted that they be treated

Danish Jews arrive in Theresienstadt. Carrying all of their belongings, they make their way into the camp. Even though these people were in the hands of the Nazis, the constant attention of their Danish comrades kept the Nazis from murdering them or transporting them to the extermination camps.

humanely. The Danish people sent care packages to the concentration camp inmates as well as letters of support, reminding them that they had not been forgotten at home. Representatives of the Danish government visited the inmates, using the services of the Swedish Red Cross to secure their admission to Theresienstadt.

In April 1945 the Theresienstadt concentration camp was emptied of its prisoners. The Jews of Denmark were the first to leave. Four hundred people were still alive and in reasonably good physical condition. A review of war records revealed that the approximately fifty Danish Jews who died in captivity had died largely of natural causes.

The Jews from the concentration camp and those who had spent the last part of the war in Sweden returned to Denmark on April 13, 1945. When they arrived in Copenhagen they found, much to their pleasure and surprise, that the population of the city had turned out to welcome them with cheers, flowers, and good wishes.

The events in Denmark in the summer of 1943 are unique in the annals of World War II. Nowhere else did a government and an entire nation register unified support on behalf of its Jewish citizens. Nowhere else did a people continue to express concern even when part of its population was interred in the German death camps. As far as is known, not a single Danish Jew died in a German gas chamber.

The people of Denmark resisted the Holocaust as a united nation in defense of their fellow citizens and in defense of their democratic traditions. When they reestablished relations with West Germany after the war, the Danes accepted Georg Duckwitz back as the German ambassador because they remembered that he too understood the importance of resistance to the Holocaust.

It is difficult to explain why the entire population of Denmark acted as it did on behalf of its Jewish citizens. Some were furious with the Germans, some acted in defense of the Danish tradition of democracy, many young people out of a love of adventure. Historian Yehuda Bauer suggests that "a whole people understood that the deportation of the Jews endangered them as socialists, Protestants, liberals, or simply as Danes."[60]

After the war, Pastor Aage Bertelsen and his wife were asked by a reporter why they had helped a student underground movement that smuggled hundreds of people to Sweden. The pastor answered simply but poignantly, "These people were in mortal danger and we had no alternative. We had to do what we did."[61]

*Our only hope will lie in the frail web of
understanding of one person for the
pain of another.*
—John Dos Passos, December 1940

The United States emerged from World War I as the most important industrial power in the world. In addition, her moral influence was so strong that President Woodrow Wilson, through the establishment of the League of Nations, essentially imposed his own views of international organization on a war-weary world. And, although the United States did not join the League, the country's influence was felt both there and throughout the Americas, where the United States largely dominated the affairs of most of Latin America.

For these reasons the refusal to aid Germany's Jews even before the Holocaust greatly influenced the attitudes adopted by other countries toward the Jews of Europe. Tragically, the perceived national interests of the United States did not appear to coincide with the needs of the Jews of Europe.

Franklin D. Roosevelt became president at a time when many influential people believed that it had been a mistake for the United States to become involved in European affairs, and consequently, in World War I. These people were called isolation-

ists. They had lobbied against further immigration and had succeeded in passing very restrictive immigration legislation in 1924.

American Anti-Semitism

Americans' dislike of foreigners fanned an increasing amount of anti-Semitism in the United States. This was fueled by the depression, which resulted in the loss of so many jobs. Americans did not want foreigners, particularly Jews from eastern Europe, coming to the country and competing for the few jobs available.

The terrible events of *Kristallnacht* in November 1938, when Jewish shops, synagogues, schools, and homes throughout Germany were set on fire and Jews were attacked and killed in the streets by Nazi thugs, did not alter these attitudes. Nor did the news that Germans were placing Jews in concentration camps in Germany, where they were brutally tortured.

The results of a series of polls taken in 1939 and 1940 reflect the generally hostile attitude of the American people toward Jews. Seventeen percent of those polled saw Jews as a menace to the United States. Another 12 to 15 percent of the population indicated that they were ready to support a campaign of anti-Semitism in the United States. An additional 20 percent were sympathetic to such a campaign while 30 percent indicated they would oppose action against Jews in the country. According to these polls, "The remainder did not care much either way."[62]

Americans read stories of Jewish persecution and for the most part ignored them or thought that they were exaggerated. Some people simply did not care. A depression-weary nation did not have the energy to worry about people in other countries, especially if those people were Jews. In addition, suggests historian David S. Wyman, "Comparatively few American non-Jews saw that the plight of the Jews was their plight too."[63] That is, they hardly understood that Hitler's attack on Jewish citizens in Germany was a threat to those moral principles on which Western civilization was based.

The suffering of impoverished Americans during the Great Depression caused many to turn a blind eye to the persecution of Europe's Jews.

In addition, many religious bigots in the United States believed that Jews must have done awful things to be the object of such terrible treatment. Many religious people in the United States still believed that all Jews deserved to suffer because they held Jews responsible for the death of Jesus of Nazareth two thousand years earlier.

For these reasons, the United States in the 1930s did not provide a bright beacon of welcome to the tormented people of Europe, especially to the Jews. The government offered a lukewarm response to an international attempt to deal with refugees in the 1930s when, for a price, Hitler was still willing to let German Jews escape.

The Evian Fiasco

In July 1938 Roosevelt indicated how he intended to respond to the plight of the Jews fleeing Germany and Austria. He sent Myron C. Taylor as the American representative at the conference at Evian, France, a resort town on the shores of Lake Geneva, to discuss the worsening refugee crisis. Speaking on behalf of Roosevelt, Taylor wistfully expressed the hope that other nations would prove to be generous and take in Jews desperate to leave Germany.

The other countries represented at Evian took their cue from the United States. Since the United States did not display great sympathy for the plight of these people, the other representatives expressed diplomatic platitudes and kept their gates shut to the doomed Jews. Four South American countries—Argentina, Chile, Uruguay, and Mexico—adopted particularly strict limitations on Jewish immigration.

The U.S. Congress did not even permit its limited legal immigration quotas to be filled. People with entry visas found it difficult to negotiate the red tape barriers

American Jews in New York protest the treatment of Jews in Hitler's Germany in 1933. Despite such protests, the U.S. government did little to aid Germany's Jewish population.

erected by Congress against their entry. People with family members in the United States, even those with sons serving in the American armed forces, were unable to gain entry. Refugee ships were turned away from the shores of the United States. Their doomed occupants were forced to return to the death camps of Europe.

Some groups and some newspapers denounced these actions. An editorial in the *Churchman* on October 1, 1940, which noted the media attacks on Jews by American hero Charles Lindbergh and Republican senator Gerald P. Nye, concluded:

Strangely enough, many otherwise decent citizens, even members of Christian churches, have fostered the Nazi-directed efforts by indulging in anti-Semitic talk. When Lindbergh came out in the open with his anti-Semitic brutality large members of such cooperators began to see the ultimate meaning and danger of such talk. It is a pity that many Christians, whose anti-Semitism has denied them their right to the name Christian, have to be awakened.[64]

Journals such as the *Nation* and *New Republic* used their front pages to publish all news they received regarding the extermination camps. Most others published limited stories which appeared on the back pages where they could be overlooked.

A Brutal Rejection

One of the more notorious cases of the United States' turning away ships filled with refugees is that of the SS *St. Louis*, which arrived off the coast of Cuba in 1939. The Cuban government refused entry to the ship's nine hundred desperate Jews. The ship then remained for a short while off the coast of Miami, Florida. Robert W. Ross quotes the *Lutheran Companion*'s account of the events in his book *So It Was True*.

As the *St. Louis* steamed out of Havana harbor, presumably to return to Hamburg, its decks were described as scenes of abject despair. Mass suicide among the passengers was predicted. Later the vessel was reported to have cast anchor three miles off shore at Miami Beach, Florida, where it was marking time while further negotiations were being conducted with the Cuban authorities in the hope that the latter might relent.

This in fact did not happen, but H. R. Hibner in the *Christian Advocate* several weeks later wrote, "I rejoice that the Jewish refugees aboard the liner *St. Louis*, compelled to return with its passengers to Europe, have been received into the Christian countries of England, France, Belgium, and Holland, and I hope and believe that if ever again a shipload of those suffering persecution enter our waters, they will not again be turned back but be wholeheartedly received by a Christian people."

Tragically, almost all of the nine hundred passengers of the SS *St. Louis* were rounded up when their countries fell to the Nazis and perished in concentration camps.

American Jewish Aid Organization

Only a tiny number of representatives in the Congress were Jewish. Among them Samuel Dickstein and Emmanuel Celler spoke out in efforts to increase rescue efforts. Their calls were not answered.

Before the United States entered World War II in late 1941 some funds found their way into Europe to assist the victims of the Nazi onslaught. Most of this money came from Jewish organizations such as the World Jewish Congress and the Joint Distribution Committee. It was distributed through the efforts of the Joint American Distribution Committee, known as the Joint. The Joint had offices in Geneva, Switzerland, and Istanbul, Turkey.

The Joint worked with the YMCA, the Quakers, the Red Cross, and other assistance organizations. These American funds were used primarily to secure places of safety for Jewish children who were left orphaned as a result of the Holocaust.

Once the United States became a participant in the war, it became illegal to send funds to German-controlled Europe. Jewish relief organizations continued to collect money in the United States and most of it found its way into the hands of rescue workers in Europe. Now, however, such organizations worked under the threat of prosecution by the American government. Their rescue efforts became more difficult. So, increasingly, they directed their efforts from neutral countries such as Switzerland and Spain, rather than France, Holland, Belgium, and elsewhere where Jews were in hiding.

Still, though restricted, those working to rescue Jews fought their limitations. Historian Leni Yahil writes that "While scrupulously observing the legality of its operations, in conformity with American law, the JDC tried to lend support to every kind of rescue action—official, secret, and even some that were illegal according to the laws and ordinances of one country to another."[65] Saving Jews was their most important consideration.

American Jews continued to try to assist their families and their coreligionists in Europe, but at home, they too felt themselves to be endangered. They knew that anti-Semitism in the United States was greater during the war than it had been before.

Many synagogues were defaced. Jewish children were taunted and beaten in American cities. The radio blasted hate-filled tirades by such fascists as Father Charles Coughlin and others who shared his racist views. An American Fascist Party, called the Silver Shirts, received support from such famous Americans as Charles Lindbergh. They held marches in several cities. They took part in large public demonstrations. The Silver Shirts made many American cities dangerous places for Jews.

In such a threatening environment at home, many American Jews found it extremely difficult to speak out on behalf of their fellow Jews in Europe. This was the case particularly before news of the gas chambers and ovens became known in the middle of 1942.

By that point it became impossible to ignore the facts of the extermination campaign Hitler and his armies waged against the Jews of Europe. News from Geneva, London, Warsaw, and elsewhere arrived at the State Department in Washington, D.C. The reports were based on information smuggled out of the death camps by survivors of the extermination campaign. They provided detailed information regarding the gassing, the shootings, the starving people, the barbed wire, the forced labor camps, and the mounds and mounds of dead, emaciated bodies. Names such as Majdanek, Treblinka, Sobibor, and Auschwitz conjured up images of torture and death.

This newspaper gives evidence to the anti-Semitic attitudes in the United States. Such attitudes assured that America did little to rescue the Jews.

State Department Hides Information

Many newspaper editorials in the United States tried to play down the enormity of the murders. A group of people at the State Department, led by Breckenridge Long, a virulent anti-Semite and nationalist, deliberately tried to hide this information entirely. Long ordered that reports from American consulates could no longer include information regarding the Holocaust. Breckenridge Long and his cohorts simply refused to concern themselves with the slaughter of innocent men, women, and children, especially if they were Jewish.

They kept the official information they received from Geneva from becoming public to help prevent open debates on the subject in Congress. Their major concern was that if news of its suppression came to the attention of influential Jews, there might be a scandal.

Paul T. Culberton of the State Department, Division of European Affairs, expressed just such an opinion: "I don't like the idea of sending this [information from Dr. Gerhart Riegner, the representative of the World Jewish Congress in Geneva about mass Jewish murders] on to [Rabbi Stephen Wise] but if the Rabbi hears later that we had the message and didn't let him in on it he might put up a kick. Why not send it on and add that the Legation [in Geneva] has no information to confirm the story."[66]

At the same time the president and his cabinet could always deny knowledge of these events. Certainly, however, the president and his immediate advisers knew about the extent of the murders through U.S. intelligence agencies. American intelligence officers such as Allen Dulles, head of the Office of Strategic Services (OSS) in Bern,

Switzerland, from 1942 to 1945, held secret meetings with members of the Abwehr, the German intelligence agency, during the course of the war.

American Goal to Win War

Roosevelt found himself in a difficult situation. He was aware of what was happening in Europe. First lady Eleanor Roosevelt urged him to take action to resist the Holocaust. Roosevelt himself had many Jewish friends and appointees.

Yet above all else Franklin Roosevelt was a politician. He would not act contrary to the views and prejudices of the political forces whose votes in Congress enabled him to wage war against Hitler. Winning World War II was his main concern. Roosevelt knew that he would lose that political support if the isolationists and anti-Semitic forces in the country believed that he was waging a war just to save the lives of Jews. For Roosevelt the most important objective in World War II was to defeat the Axis powers, Germany, Japan, and Italy. They had to be defeated in order to defend the interests of the United States.

Roosevelt had additional obligations. For instance, he had an important agreement with Winston Churchill, prime minister of Great Britain, which spelled out their joint war aims. The two leaders agreed that World War II would be fought until Germany surrendered unconditionally. That meant that no special deals could be made with anti-Hitler factions in Germany, even if that meant saving the lives of Jews in the concentration camps.

The Soviet Union, the wartime ally of the United States and Great Britain, understood the policy of unconditional surrender of Germany to be absolute and final. Any change in that policy might drive the Soviet

President Franklin Roosevelt (left) and Winston Churchill, prime minister of England, made an agreement to fight Germany until Germany unconditionally surrendered. This war aim took precedence over helping save European Jews.

Union into signing a separate peace treaty with Germany. If that happened, the United States and Great Britain might even lose the war.

So, in response to appeals by American Jews to resist the Holocaust, the American government had a ready answer. The faster Germany was defeated, the government maintained, the faster Jewish lives would be saved.

Many people, particularly the Jewish youth fighters in Hungary, sent messages urging the United States to bomb the concentration camps and the railroad lines leading to them. The government, however, left that decision in the hands of the military authori-ties, who determined that only considerations of military necessity, not humanitarian concerns for Jews, should influence the location of air strikes in Europe.

The United States also refused to engage in discussions toward the end of 1943 that might have resulted in the saving of hundreds of thousands of Jews. At that time some unusual and secret talks took place between representatives of Heinrich Himmler and people close to humanitarian groups in the United States. Himmler saw that the war would be lost and considered himself the natural successor of a defeated Hitler.

Heinrich Himmler inspects SS troops. Himmler tried to make a deal with the Allies: 1 million Hungarian Jews in exchange for military equipment to fight the Russians.

Himmler needed tens of thousands of trucks to continue his efforts against the Russians, whom he feared far more than he did the West. Himmler also understood that if such a deal could be made, the alliance between the United States and Britain on the one hand and the Soviet Union on the other would be threatened. Joseph Stalin surely would have regarded such a deal as a threat to his own country.

The highly secret conversations dealt with the possibility of releasing 1 million Hungarian Jews in exchange for the trucks as well as other military equipment urgently needed by the German army. This equipment, the Germans promised to various secret agents, would of course only be used against the Russians, not against the armies of the Western powers.

There was to be no deal. The transfer of money to Europe became even more difficult. Funds then available in Switzerland for humanitarian purposes were frozen to avoid any appearance of dealing with the Germans. In fact the United States even reported the talks to Stalin in Russia to avoid the appearance of taking action behind his back. Besides, it was not clear that any country was interested in taking in a million Jews.

Given all these circumstances, it is possible to understand why no massive acts of resistance to the Holocaust in the United States occurred. However, many organizations and many thousands of men and women did what they could to relieve the suffering of the Jews in Europe. The Quakers and the Red Cross, for example, made great but largely futile efforts to bring children to the United States.

Role of Rabbi Stephen Wise

Many American Jews did speak up. The American Jewish press actively urged the government to resist the Holocaust. So too did the American Jewish Congress, the World Jewish Congress, the Union of Orthodox Rabbis, the Jewish Labor Committee, and the American Jewish Committee. Reform rabbi Stephen S. Wise, a longtime activist in the social justice movement and the most important American spokesman for Zionism, never ceased his efforts.

Rabbi Wise first began to organize an American movement to boycott German goods in 1933 in response to early German outrages against German Jews. The American Jewish Congress continued to press for such a boycott and by 1937 Wise was able to gain the support of American trade unions for a mass rally in Madison Square Garden in New York. Addressing a crowd consisting of both Jews and non-Jews, Wise declared: "The Boycott, moral and economic, is a warless war against the war makers. The Jews in Germany were but one element of the civilization that Nazism had sworn to destroy."[67]

Many left-wing organizations in the United States, including trade unions, socialist groups, and communist organizations, encouraged the government to speak up on behalf of the tormented people in Europe. And many public personalities such as William Randolph Hearst openly and continually spoke out. But they represented a tiny fraction of the population. Their words and actions fell on a government resistant to such pressures.

Finally, a small group of brave men within the Treasury Department decided to challenge the government's decision not to act on behalf of Europe's Jews. These men detested the efforts of Breckenridge Long and his group to subvert the Constitution of the United States by withholding information from the president and by making foreign policy instead of Congress. The group included John W. Pehle, Raymond Paul,

Those Christian Saps

The following poem, published in a 1943 *Common Ground*, demonstrates clearly the brutal anti-Semitism with which American Jews had to contend.

From the shores of Coney Island
Looking out into the sea,
Stands a kosher air-raid warden,
Wearing V for victory,
     who chants:
Let those Christian saps, go fight
     the Japs,
In the uniform we're made.
. . . So it's onward into battle,
Let us send the Christian slobs.
When the war is done and Victory
     won,
All us Jews will have their jobs.

A Tragic Fate Goes Unnoticed

Rabbi Stephen Wise was one of the leading spokesmen for American Jews during World War II. He found that many newspapers tried to diminish the magnitude of the plight of European Jews. The following letter, which Rabbi Wise sent to the *Christian Century* in January 1943, expresses clearly his anger and frustration. The letter is quoted in Robert W. Ross's *So It Was True*.

It would appear that you are more interested in seeking to prove that figures which I gave out in the name of five important Jewish organizations of America are inaccurate in respect to Jewish mass massacres in the Hitler-occupied countries than you are in making clear to American Christians how unspeakable has been the conduct of Hitlerism against the Jewish people.

Whether this [the anti-Semitic position of the *Christian Century*] is merely a reflection of a personal Judeophobia on the part of the editor, or whether it conveys the considerable attitude of the editorial board of the *Christian Century* is not for me to say. Christian ministers with whom I have discussed the problem have felt your article reflected the subconscious desire not so much to express compassion for the victims of Hitlerism as to shield Hitler from the consequences of his crime. I confess that I cannot quite understand that you should seem to be spiritually unconcerned about the tragic fate of the people whose gift to the world you propose to revere and worship.

Rabbi Stephen Wise delivers an address at an anti-Nazi protest demonstration in New York in 1937.

and Joshua E. Dubois Jr. They were all non-Jews who endangered their own careers in the interests of a principle. That principle was their refusal to permit the officials of the State Department to thwart the policies of the American government.

All these men had information regarding the restriction of relief funds which could be sent to Europe. They came to believe that the U.S. State Department was "guilty not only of gross procrastination and willful failure to act, but even of willful attempts to prevent action from being taken to rescue Jews from Hitler."[68] During 1943 they spent many months searching government files for documents that would reveal the way in which Long suppressed information. When they had amassed considerable incriminating evidence, they took their report to Henry Morgenthau, the secretary of the treasury. The title of the report was "Report to the Secretary on the Acquiescence of This Government in the Murder of the Jews."

Morgenthau was the highest-ranking Jew in the Roosevelt administration. He read the report and immediately made an appointment to speak to the president. On January 17, 1944, he told Roosevelt that unless the president acted on behalf of the remnant of the Jewish population in Europe, he, Morgenthau, would reveal to the press the details of the report indicating corruption was rampant in the State Department.

Roosevelt knew that Morgenthau would carry out his threat. The president also knew that the war was coming to an end. And he sensed that in the United States, the attitude of the American people toward the suffering of the Jews of Europe was beginning to turn. The grim reports and photographs sent to the United States by escapees of the camps and by the Jewish Palestinian organization Yishuv, had been verified to the satisfaction of most Americans and many began to want to help the Jews.

On January 22, 1944, Franklin Roosevelt signed an order establishing the War Relief Board, or WRB. The board was ordered to "take all measures . . . consistent with the successful prosecution of the war . . . to rescue the victims of enemy oppression."[69] The board had the authority to engage in all measures of relief, including negotiations with the enemy if necessary in order to save lives. At long last, and almost too late, the government of the United States took active steps to resist the Holocaust.

Roswell D. McClelland became the main representative of the WRB, centered

Henry Morgenthau Jr. was instrumental in revealing the ways that government officials hid information about the Holocaust from the American public and Roosevelt.

in Bern, Switzerland. McClelland immediately established contacts with the International Red Cross, the Swedish government, and the Vatican in Rome in an effort to save the last remaining sizable Jewish population in Europe, the Jews of Hungary.

At the same time, Zionists in the United States sensed that politicians of both major political parties were willing to turn their support to the establishment of a Jewish national homeland. Nineteen forty-four was an election year and the Jewish vote in many large cities was important. Both Roosevelt and the Republican candidate for the presidency, Thomas Dewey, pledged their strong support for a Jewish homeland in Palestine.

At the political conventions held that summer both parties included support for unrestricted Jewish immigration into Palestine as a plank in their platforms. Coming very late in the game, too late to save the lives of 6 million slaughtered people, in 1944 the United States finally made effective gestures toward assisting the survivors of the Holocaust.

I'd never be able to go back to Stockholm without knowing that I'd done all a man could do to save as many Jews as possible.

—Raoul Wallenberg

At the beginning of World War II about three-quarters of a million Jews lived in Hungary. About half of them lived in Budapest, the capital of the country, the rest in small towns and villages. Hungary entered World War II on the side of Germany in order to protect its territory. The alliance continued until 1944. So Hitler allowed Hungary to control its own internal affairs. This included matters relating to its large Jewish population. The Germans urged the Hungarian government to deport its Jews, but the Hungarian government did not comply. The Hungarian government, like most other governments in eastern Europe, passed drastic anti-Semitic legislation during the 1930s. Much of it was designed either to please Germany, the dominant power in the region, or to steal Jewish property.

However, most of Hungary's anti-Semitic laws were not enforced. The Hungarians practiced what might be called a polite form of anti-Semitism. Since many prominent Jews were members of the nobility, and owned and directed most of Hungary's major industries, their presence, their skills, and their international trading and banking connections constituted the backbone of the Hungarian economy. Historian Kati Marton remarks:

> Until the mid-forties, Hungarian anti-Semitism retained its well-defined, almost polite quality. It was as much a part of the Hungarian gentleman's wardrobe as the starched front shirt he wore to the premiere of the Vienna Opera season. But by 1944 he was no longer in control of what constituted the acceptable level of Jew-hating.[70]

As the quotation suggests, a very ambiguous situation existed in Hungary. The Jews of Hungary felt insulated by their great economic importance to the country. However, the prominence of so many Jews prompted jealousy and greed in less affluent, non-Jewish Hungarians whose economic situation continued to worsen as the war progressed. It was precisely these people who took the anti-Semitic propaganda of the Hungarian government seriously. They joined the fascist and extremely anti-Semitic Arrow Cross Party in large numbers and constituted a growing menace to the Jewish population of Hungary.

The Jews of Hungary   89

The Politics of Hungary

The Jews of Hungary were unprepared to resist the Holocaust en masse in part because they considered themselves an essential element in Hungarian society. This attitude was fostered by an existing regime that stated one policy but practiced another. Historian Leni Yahil, in *The Holocaust*, quotes Hungarian historian Bela Vago, who describes this paradoxical situation.

This was one of the paradoxical phenomena of the Hungarian regime which contained a mixture of vestiges of feudalism with democratic-parliamentary elements, the authoritarianism of a quasi-fascist regime with tolerance toward the democratic opposition; an official anti-Semitic policy with tolerance towards Jews in the fields of journalism, the arts, and other areas of culture. The Jews could be active as members of Parliament until the German occupation in 1944.

Hungary Tries to Break Alliance with Germany

The situation became increasingly dangerous in 1944. Admiral Miklos Horthy headed the government of Hungary. The career politician knew that it was only a matter of time before the Allies overran Germany. He decided that it was time to break his ties with the Nazis. And so he began secret negotiations with the Allies to withdraw from the war before Russian troops conquered Hungary.

Hitler acted quickly once he learned of Horthy's plans to defect. On March 19, 1944, German troops suddenly invaded and took over Hungary. Under the direction of Adolf Eichmann, the Germans, who were well assisted by thousands of Arrow Cross members, began to round up Hungarian Jews, primarily in rural areas, and deport them to concentration camps for extermination.

The Arrow Cross were eager to help the German forces. The Germans further whetted the enthusiasm of its members for blood by promising to give them a large share of the property that they could extort from the Jews they caught. Horthy's government did not protest or take steps to halt the early roundups. The Arrow Cross, therefore, cooperated willingly and without government hindrance with Adolf Eichmann's expedited extermination plans.

The anti-Semitic Arrow Cross were not the only ones who cooperated with the Germans. Urbanized Jews in Hungary, promised by Eichmann exemption from deportation, did nothing when the Jews in the provincial towns were rounded up and deported. They continued to deceive themselves when the Germans began to act against the Jews of the capital. Many still cooperated even when they themselves were deported. They kept hoping until the very end that Horthy would protect them.

The leader of the Hungarian Jewish community and the head of the Hungarian *Judenrat*, Samu Stern, also cooperated. Eichmann promised the rich and prominent businessman and his committee that if the Jews of Budapest cooperated, they would be safe. Andreus Biss, a Jew who lived in Budapest during these terrible days, wrote that it was the job of the Jewish council

Miklos Horthy (right) rejected German pressure to impose harsher measures on the Jews. Nevertheless, soldiers of the anti-Semitic Arrow Cross (below) managed to deport many Hungarian Jews to Auschwitz.

merely to "see that calm reigned and order was maintained during the deportations."[71]

The Jews of Hungary were utterly dumbstruck by the sudden change in their fortunes. They had always placed their fate in the belief that Horthy would continue to protect them as he had in the past. They made no plans for their own defense. Nor did they have the ability to protect themselves.

Jewish Community Tries to Ignore Danger

Like Jews elsewhere, those in Hungary tried to ignore the news from Poland and Russia because it was too horrible to contemplate. When ghettoization began in April in the rural districts, the Jews of Budapest believed that only a few would be taken. When the trains began leaving for the extermination camps on May 15, 1944, many people continued to believe that their coreligionists merely were being resettled.

Zionists in Hungary

The only resistance to the Holocaust that emerged in Hungary came from two sources. One element was the small local Zionist Party. The party was led by an engineer named

Jewish deportees march down a main street in Hungary on their way to deportation to Auschwitz concentration camp.

Pray That We Shall Die

The Jews of Hungary were rounded up and squeezed into all sorts of holding centers. One of fifteen thousand internees who were locked in a brickyard managed to smuggle out the following letter, quoted in Wyman's *The Abandonment of the Jews: America and the Holocaust.*

I am afraid I cannot stand it for long, for we are suffering beyond descrip-tion. We lie in the dust, have neither straw-mattresses nor covers, and will freeze to death. The place is sealed. I do not see any way out. . . . We are so neglected that we do not look human any more. There is no possibility for cleaning anything. We have not taken off our clothes since coming here. Best greetings to you all, pray for us that we shall die soon.

Otto Komoly, assisted by Reszo Kasztner and Samuel Springmann. These men were detested by the established Jews of Budapest. They were viewed as troublemakers for warning of the impending danger and as zealots for discussing Zionist subjects. In the recent past they had even been banned from the synagogues because they had dared to discuss Zionism.

The second source of resistance came from a small group of young Jewish refugees who had escaped the deportations in Poland and Slovakia. These young people, too, were Zionists. Most of them had no family members remaining alive. They were dedicated to helping as many people as possible escape and find their way to Palestine. When outside help came for the Jews of Hungary, the combined experience of the Zionists helped facilitate the work of the world relief organizations.

The young Jewish resistance fighters worked independently but they acknowledged Komoly and his associates as the leaders of Zionist activities. Together the two groups formed a loose organization called the Relief and Rescue Committee comprising all Zionists groups operating in Hungary. The committee ultimately would save the majority of Jews who survived in Hungary into 1945.

But like the local Zionists, the young foreigners were not supported by the local Jewish population. Samu Stern and his upper-class associates regarded the political views of the young resistance fighters from Poland and Slovakia with distaste. They saw no reason to work with these foreign-looking youngsters with whom they could not identify. They also did not want to believe the dire warnings of the young people and the stories they told about what had happened to their families in Poland and Slovakia.

Role of the Yishuv

Fortunately, however, the Relief and Rescue Committee received assistance and financial support from the Yishuv in Constantinople,

A man on the street in Budapest wears a yellow star to distinguish him as a Jew. Once the Germans occupied Budapest, they began to impose anti-Semitic restrictions.

The Jews of Hungary   93

Turkey. The Yishuv, headed by Moshe Krausz, was the name of the organization that represented the Jewish population of Palestine. At that time the entire Jewish population of Palestine was smaller than that of pre-war Warsaw, fewer than 500,000. But the population was relatively young and many had gained military experience through association with the British occupation forces during the 1930s and 1940s. They undertook daring tasks to smuggle out as many Jews as possible from fortress Europe with money, advice, and occasional military contingents. As the crisis deepened for Hungarian Jews, Moshe Krausz set up his office in a building called the Glass House in central Budapest so that he could help to coordinate rescue efforts on the spot.

The Glass House, which was donated to the rescue workers by the rich Hungarian Jew Arthur Weisz, eventually came under the protection of the Swiss government. Consequently, the hundreds of Jews who ultimately sought safety there had some protection from capture.

By the middle of 1944, when the German occupation sealed all escape routes, the resistance fighters had succeeded in getting several thousand Jews across the border from Hungary into Romania. The Zionists led the *tiyul*, or excursion, which brought escapees to the Romanian border, where highly paid guides led Jewish refugees into Romania. There other Zionists helped them continue their journey to Palestine.

The German takeover of Hungary closed the escape routes across Hungary's borders. The Zionists reexamined their options. They decided that revolt was impossible. They were few in number and they had only a handful of weapons. In addition, the Hungarian population generally was hostile to Jews and would not support a Jewish uprising against the German occupation forces. They certainly did not have the support of the *Judenrat*. So they turned their efforts toward helping to save the lives of as many Hungarian Jews as possible through other means.

The one very special skill they had for this work was their ability to forge documents. They operated several small secret printing presses in Budapest. They turned out birth certificates, baptismal certificates, driver's licenses, and lodging and ration cards. Foremost among the document makers was Shraga Weil, who later became one of Israel's best-known painters.

Once they were armed with these identification papers, many of the Jewish youth group members were able to move about relatively freely in Hungary. Many of them could pass as non-Jews.

At first the young people printed enough "official documents" to supply all members of the youth organizations who wanted to participate in the resistance work. Then they turned out thousands of other pieces of "official identification" for those people they persuaded to resist the roundups.

They established bunkers for their own living arrangements. They also created safe houses where members of the group could hide in case of danger or where they could bring other Jews whom they had rescued. In doing this, they established a pattern of resistance which later became part of an international effort to save Hungarian Jews.

Some of the more "Hungarian-looking" members of the youth groups went out to the provinces to warn Jews not to show up when the Germans came to deport them. They also tried to bring young native Hungarian Zionists back with them to Budapest where their chances of survival were greater than in the small towns.

Unfortunately, few people in the provinces listened to the resistance fighters. Even many of the young Hungarian Zionists decided to share the fate of their families in the "resettlement" rather than join the resistance groups in Budapest.

They were doomed. Eichmann and his assistants worked so quickly that in less than three months the only Jews left in Hungary were the approximately 190,000 people who lived in the capital. Between May 15 and July 8, 1944, the Germans sent 148 trains, loaded with 450,000 Jews, to the concentration camps.

The Jews of Budapest were somewhat more fortunate than those who had lived in the provinces. At about the time that the roundup of the Hungarian Jews began the world suddenly awakened to the catastrophe overtaking this last remaining Jewish population in Europe.

World Aids Remaining Jews

Reporters who experienced the liberation of the first concentration camps sent back ghastly pictures of the consequences of human depravity. The piles of human skeletons, the mountains of eyeglasses and human hair could not be explained away. Moreover, with the defeat of Germany now virtually certain, government leaders wanted to present themselves as the upholders of such Western democratic traditions as humanity, charity, and concern for the suffering of their fellows.

President Roosevelt of the United States; Pope Pius XII; Frederick Borne, the head of the International Red Cross; the Orthodox Church in Hungary; and King Gustav of Sweden spoke out against the deportations. American pilots bombed Budapest. President Roosevelt warned the leaders of Hungary that they would be punished after the war for their crimes if they did not stop cooperating with the Germans.

Partly in response to this worldwide clamor, Horthy announced the end of the deportations of Jews. Adolf Eichmann was infuriated and vowed that he would resume his unfinished task.

Near the time that the deportations stopped, international rescue efforts began. The Jews of provincial Hungary were gone. Perhaps something could be done to save those who still were alive in the capital. WRB representatives made contact with neutral countries to assist in this rescue work. Chief among these countries was Sweden.

Raoul Wallenberg

King Gustav gave permission for a well-connected Swede, Raoul Wallenberg, to undertake relief efforts in Hungary on behalf of the War Relief Board. The thirty-one-year-old Wallenberg arrived in Budapest on July 16, 1944. The young diplomat was full of enthusiasm for his task. His pockets were full of the money that had come from the WRB in the United States and he also had received authority to use any means possible to save the remnant of the Jewish community of Hungary. He arrived with official papers naming him a member of the Swedish embassy staff in Budapest. This status provided him with diplomatic immunity as a cover for his activities.

The temporary lull in the deportations in July gave Wallenberg an opportunity to assess the situation. He found that the youth groups already had set up food kitchens and nurseries for orphans. He also found that the international community in Budapest had begun to issue all sorts of semiofficial

Raoul Wallenberg went to Budapest in 1944 to help protect the nearly 190,000 Jews who remained in the capital after the initial deportations.

the neutrals announced that these buildings, called yellow star buildings because of the markings painted on them, were the legal property of the countries involved. They thus should be safe from trespass, just as were their official embassy buildings.

Wallenberg enlarged and reorganized these operations. He worked closely with the International Red Cross to issue large numbers of official documents to Jews who had the most remote connection with anyone in Sweden. Soon all pretense of relatedness was dropped. He extended diplomatic immunity to all sorts of buildings in the Hungarian capital, thus making them somewhat safe from the Hungarian fascists who continued to make life a living hell for the Jews in Budapest.

Wallenberg worked particularly closely with the young Jewish resistance workers who provided him with the organization which he lacked. He hired hundreds of Jews to work with him. This meant that they no longer had to wear the yellow identity badge on their clothing. His staff could move freely around the city. They brought him information and they supplied him with many papers which he himself could not obtain. They also acted as a kind of protection force for the young Swedish diplomat, who increasingly incurred the anger of the Hungarian fascists.

papers to Jews who came to their doors. Ivar Danielsson, the Swedish ambassador, had issued seven hundred visas for Jews before Wallenberg arrived in Hungary.

The Swiss, Spanish, and Portuguese governments, as well as the Vatican, were willing to provide additional papers to desperate people seeking protection. Once Jews had these visas they no longer were required to wear the yellow star, which identified them as hunted people. They were under the protection of the countries that had issued their visas

Nevertheless, while these neutral countries were willing to issue visas and passports, they were not willing to take the Jews into their countries. Instead, they established their legal jurisdiction over specific buildings in the center of the capital. Then

Arrow Cross Government in Hungary

Amid this chaos, the Horthy government was overthrown in October. Helped by the Germans, the Arrow Cross leader, Ferenc Szalasi replaced Horthy and resumed the war.

The Szalasi period was the most dangerous time for the Jewish survivors in Budapest. Young bands of Arrow Cross thugs roamed the streets, searching for Jews to rob and murder. They frequently attempted raids on the houses under diplomatic protection as well as against the central ghetto in Budapest, established at the end of the year, which housed nearly seventy thousand people.

At this time nearly nineteen hundred houses were packed tightly with Jews living under the protection of foreign legations. In addition, thirty houses run by Jewish doctors, nurses, and some volunteer adults protected orphans. The people could only leave their houses for limited periods of time. The presence of the Arrow Cross gangs roaming through the city at will without any central governmental control made it nearly impossible for the people in these houses to obtain what they needed.

In the midst of all of this, Adolf Eichmann returned to the city. He knew that he had limited time to complete his task of extermination. Two Russian armies, led by Marshal Tolbukhin and Marshal Malinovsky, were approaching the capital.

The Jewish population of Budapest now was divided in two: those living in the yellow star houses under the protection of the various neutral legations, and about seventy thousand other people placed in extremely crowded quarters and theoretically under the protection of the international community. This ghetto period for Hungarian Jews lasted only a very short time.

Eichmann was determined to carry out his plans for extermination. By the end of 1944 he had few cattle cars available for deportation. Instead, he gathered the elderly and sick from the large international ghetto and began a forced march hundreds of miles to Germany. Most of them died along the way.

Charles Lutz, the head of the Swiss legation in Budapest, describes the places where these people were gathered:

Death Marches

Even in the last days before the Red Army overran Hungary, the German occupation was determined to kill as many Jews as possible. In *Memorandum Concerning the Situation of the Hungarian Jews*, quoted in Bent's *Wallenberg, Letters and Dispatches*, Raoul Wallenberg describes the harrowing scenes of these last murders.

Probably in the neighborhood of 40,000 Jews, of whom 15,000 men from the Labor Service and 25,000 of both sexes seized in their homes or in the street, have been forced to march on foot to Germany. It is a distance of 240 kilometers. The weather has been cold and rainy ever since these death marches began. They have had to sleep under rain shelters and in the open. Most have only been given something to eat or drink three or four times. Many have died. I learned in Mosonmagyarovar that 7 persons had died that day, and 7 persons the day before. The Portuguese secretary to the legation had observed 42 dead persons along the route, and Deputy Prime Minister Szalasi admitted to me that he had seen 2 dead. Those who were too tired to walk were shot. On the border, they were received with kicks and blows by the Eichmann Special SS Command and were taken away to hard labor on the border fortifications.

Their condition may not be compared to persons afflicted by any other spiritual distress or human sufferings. Poverty and pain will still leave a man his dignity if there remains security based on law. But human dignity vanishes in the event of a total deprivation of rights and total defenselessness.[72]

This was the situation faced by Wallenberg and the young Jewish resistance in October 1944. Fortunately, prewar food magnates helped supply food to the safe houses and even to the large ghetto. Jewish spies wearing the uniform of the Arrow Cross found out about planned attacks and forced marches and warned Wallenberg, then raced to defend the victims of the attacks.

Use of False Documents

Sometimes Wallenberg was able to extract people from the marches by handing them Swedish "passports." Sometimes, however, Wallenberg and the Jewish resistance arrived too late to prevent the Arrow Cross from pulling children from their houses and murdering them in the streets. Often they arrived at the Danube River too late to prevent the Hungarian fascists from stripping Jews of their clothing, shooting them, and throwing their naked bodies into the river.

Wallenberg himself dashed from one scene of disaster to another. He challenged Arrow Cross mobs and even German military detachments and convinced many to relinquish their victims. Pcr Anger, a member of the Swedish embassy staff, describes such a scene:

> The Germans were taken by surprise, and right under their noses, Wallenberg pulled out a large number of Jews. Many of them had no passport at all, only various papers in the Hungarian language—drivers licenses, vaccination records, or tax receipt—that the Germans did not understand. The bluff succeeded.[73]

Wallenberg even managed to stave off a final assault on the central ghetto as the Russians were approaching and Arrow Cross thugs hastily tried to kill the surviving Jews. He threatened General Schmidthuber that unless he prevented an attack "Wallenberg would make sure Schmidthuber swung on the gallows."[74]

As a result of Wallenberg's efforts, the young resistance fighters, and other international efforts, the majority of the Jewish population of Budapest survived the war. This rescue operation was the largest resistance operation to occur in Europe during World War II.

After the war many of the Zionists saw their dreams come true. They went to Palestine. They fought in the war of independence and they helped to establish the State of Israel.

As for Raoul Wallenberg, the Russian conquerors of Budapest regarded him as a U.S. spy. The funds he and the youth organizations used came largely from American-Jewish organizations. He was taken to Russia and disappeared while in detention. His fate is unknown.

Conclusions

When bad men combine, the good must associate; else they will fall, one by one, an unpitied sacrifice in a contemptible struggle.

—Edmund Burke

It is extremely difficult to draw any overall conclusions or to make any definitive statements about the extent or the effectiveness of the resistance to the Holocaust during World War II. The examples of resistance in the preceding chapters only begin to describe the numerous official and private efforts to save lives. Many incidents are lost to history forever because those who attempted to resist were destroyed in the process.

What is certain is that the lives of 6 million European Jews were destroyed. The psychotic ravings of a powerful leader fed into the long-held anti-Semitism of thousands of other Europeans whose greed and brutality betrayed the fundamental principles of Western, liberal, democratic traditions.

Yet, it is also important to remember that those who resisted or attempted to resist the Holocaust, believed in adhering to the basic tenets of their religions, of Western civilization, of basic morality. It is important, for example, to remember that the Italian army made great efforts to save the Jews who, through conquest, fell under its control in 1939 and 1940. In Italy itself, the Italian people had no interest in persecuting their fellow citizens. They made successful efforts to save the majority of Italian Jews when Germany took over Italy in 1943.

Italian Jews themselves entered the resistance movement in large numbers. At least five won the highest medals for bravery that the Italian government offers; many others worked in Allied intelligence units.

Many Romanian Jews were saved. Although the Bulgarian government of King Boris agreed to take part in the deportations of Bulgarian Jews, he somehow managed to evade doing so.

Although French Jews constituted only 1 percent of the population, they made up nearly 20 percent of the resistance movement in the country. They played a substantial role in assisting the Allied landing in North Africa; more than half of the fighters who were involved in the action were Jews. They were among the leaders of the spy ring known as the Red Orchestra, which provided information that helped clear the way for the final Allied assault at Normandy.

French Jews became a fighting force under the banner of the Organization Juive de Combat, the OJC. The OJC was responsible for nearly two thousand separate actions against German forces in France. It played a role in saving the lives of seven thousand children. Groups in Paris, Grenoble, Marseilles, and Toulouse harassed and sabotaged the Gestapo throughout the German occupation.

In the United States internal politics and religious intolerance made it difficult for the government openly to assist the Jews of Europe. Yet Jewish organizations were able to develop sympathy within the country and in Congress for the Zionist cause. This sympathy ultimately developed into successful support for the establishment of the State of Israel. Without American support it is unlikely that Israel would have gained its independence.

At the same time, young Jews from the United States enlisted in all branches of the armed forces to fight against Hitler. The military cemeteries in Europe testify to their willingness to resist the Holocaust.

Jews took part in partisan movements all over Europe. Apart from those efforts in the forest of the north, Jews were active in the partisan movements in Italy, Greece, and Bulgaria. Almost all the doctors who worked in the various Yugoslavian resistance units were Jews. Often they received supplies and assistance from Jewish paratroopers, whom the Yishuv flew into all parts of Europe to keep alive the spirit of the fighters.

Four officers of the French resistance pose in the field. Jews participated in many different resistance groups throughout Europe.

And the efforts of those doomed Jews in the ghettos and the concentration camps cannot be forgotten. Armed resistance to the Nazis took place in scores of ghettos despite the resisters' knowing that they would perish. And in Treblinka, Sachsenhausen, Sobibor, Auschwitz, and elsewhere, Jews continued the struggle against the Nazis.

Jewish Uprisings

In Auschwitz the inmates achieved a spectacular success. On October 6, 1944 they found a way to blow up crematorium number three, destroying the installation and killing many SS men. Although many tried to flee the camp after the explosion, all the Jews who escaped were captured and killed.

A photograph of four members of the Jewish resistance that fought in the Warsaw ghetto uprising.

The Jews of Palestine contributed to the rescue of thousands of their coreligionists. In the frantic days of 1939 and 1940, when it was still possible to escape from Europe, young Palestinian Jews came to Europe, begged or borrowed money with which to rent or buy ships, and worked frantically to smuggle tens of thousands of European Jews into Palestine. By March 1941 they had succeeded in hiring twenty-three ships extraditing 10,628 refugees to Palestine.

The Yishuv set up offices in Europe and provided assistance to resistance workers in many countries. It engaged in efforts to obtain accurate information regarding what the Nazis actually were doing in the conquered territories. It even engaged in conversations and attempted to make deals with the Abwehr, the German military counter-intelligence, and with Heinrich Himmler himself, when it believed that such negotiations might result in the saving of lives.

Political, economic, social, religious, geographic, and historical differences help to account for the ways in which different people and different countries resisted the Holocaust. We cannot know how we might have behaved under the circumstances that engulfed Europe during World War II. What is certain is that it is important to remember these events. It is important to pay tribute to all of these people, Jews and Gentiles alike, who resisted the efforts of Adolf Hitler and attempted to save lives. As the Talmud says, he who saves a single life, saves the entire world.

Notes

Introduction: Hitler's Objectives

1. Yehuda Bauer, *Jews for Sale? Nazi-Jewish Negotiations, 1933–1945.* New Haven, CT: Yale University Press, 1994, p. 60.
2. Yehuda Bauer, *The Jewish Emergence from Powerlessness.* Toronto: University of Toronto Press, 1979, p.38.

Chapter 1: Resistance in the Ghettos

3. Israel Gutman, *Resistance: The Warsaw Ghetto Uprising.* New York: Houghton Mifflin, 1994, p. 59.
4. Lucy Dawidowicz, *The War Against the Jews.* New York: Holt, Rinehart, and Winston, 1975, p. 4.
5. Bauer, *The Jewish Emergence from Powerlessness*, p. 245.
6. Quoted in Joe J. Heydecker, *The Warsaw Ghetto: A Photographic Record 1941–1944.* London: I. B. Tauris, 1990, p. 4.
7. Quoted in Dawidowicz, *The War Against the Jews*, p. 220.
8. Quoted in Michael Berenbaum, *The World Must Know: The History of the Holocaust as Told in the United States Holocaust Memorial Museum.* Boston: Little, Brown, 1993, p. 82.
9. Quoted in Berenbaum, *The World Must Know*, p. 83.
10. Quoted in Dawidowicz, *The War Against the Jews*, p. 143.
11. Bauer, *The Jewish Emergence from Powerlessness*, p. 177.

12. Quoted in Berenbaum, *The World Must Know*, p. 93.

Chapter 2: The Warsaw Ghetto Uprising

13. Gutman, *Resistance*, p. xiv.
14. Yitzhak Zuckerman, *A Surplus of Memory: Chronicle of the Warsaw Ghetto Uprising.* Berkeley and Los Angeles: University of California Press, 1993, p. xiii.
15. Dawidowicz, *The War Against the Jews*, p. 334.
16. Zuckerman, *A Surplus Of Memory*, p. 209.
17. Quoted by Israel Gutman, "The Genesis of the Resistance in the Warsaw Ghetto," in Michael R. Marrus, ed., *The Nazi Holocaust: Jewish Resistance to the Holocaust*, vol. 7. Westport, CT: Meckler, 1989, p. 135.
18. Israel Gutman, "Youth Movements in the Underground and the Ghetto Revolts," in Marrus, *The Nazi Holocaust*, vol. 7, p. 181.
19. Quoted in Gutman, *Resistance*, p. 207.
20. Quoted in Gutman, *Resistance*, p. 209.
21. Quoted in Heydecker, *The Warsaw Ghetto*, p. 17.
22. Quoted in Heydecker, *The Warsaw Ghetto*, p. 18.
23. Isaac Kowalski, ed., *Anthology of Armed Jewish Resistance 1939–1945.* Brooklyn: Jewish Combatants Publishing House, 1992, p. 47.
24. Kowalski, *Anthology of Armed Jewish Resistance*, p. 47.

Chapter 3: Escape to the Forests

25. Shalom Cholawski, *Soldiers from the Ghetto*. London: Nativity Press, 1980, p. 84.
26. Quoted in Dov Levin, *Fighting Back: Lithuanian Jewry's Armed Resistance to the Nazis, 1941–1945*. New York: Homes & Meier, 1985, p. 77.
27. Levin, *Fighting Back*, p. 153.
28. Quoted in Shalom Cholawski, "The Judenrat in Minsk," in Marrus, *The Nazi Holocaust*.
29. Yuri Suhl, "The Resistance Movement in the Ghetto of Minsk," in Marrus, *The Nazi Holocaust*, vol. 7, p. 117.
30. Levin, *Fighting Back*, p. 199.
31. Yitzhak Arad, "Jewish Family Camps in the Forests—An Original Means of Rescue," in Marrus, *The Nazi Holocaust*, vol. 7, p. 231.
32. Cholawski, *Soldiers from the Ghetto*, p. 177.

Chapter 4: Holland

33. Miep Gies, *Anne Frank Remembered*. New York: Simon and Schuster, 1987, p. 40.
34. Louis de Jong, "Jews and Non-Jews in Nazi-Occupied Holland," in Marrus, *The Nazi Holocaust*, vol. 4, p. 130.
35. de Jong, "Jews and Non-Jews in Nazi-Occupied Holland," in Marrus, *The Nazi Holocaust*, vol. 4, p. 135.
36. Gies, *Anne Frank Remembered*, p. 87.
37. Quoted in Berenbaum, *The World Must Know*, p. 71.
38. Quoted in Russell Misser, ed., *The Resistance*. New York: Time-Life Books, 1979, p. 130.
39. Haim Avni, "The Zionist Underground in Holland and France and the Escape to Spain," in Marrus, *The Nazi Holocaust*, vol. 7, p. 511.
40. Gies, *Anne Frank Remembered*, p. 110.

Chapter 5: Le Chambon-sur-Lignon

41. Pierre Sauvage, in the film *Weapons of the Spirit*.
42. Philip P. Hallie, *Lest Innocent Blood Be Shed: The Story of the Village of Le Chambon and How Goodness Happened There*. New York: Harper & Row, 1979, p. 34.
43. Quoted in Sauvage, *Weapons of the Spirit*.
44. Milton Meltzer, *Rescue: The Story of How Gentiles Saved Jews in the Holocaust*. New York: Harper & Row, 1988, p. 71.
45. Conversation with Nellie Trocmé Hewitt, February 1997, in St. Paul, Minnesota.
46. Conversation with Nellie Trocmé Hewitt, February 1997, in St. Paul, Minnesota.
47. Quoted in Sauvage, *Weapons of the Spirit*.
48. Conversation with Nellie Trocmé Hewitt, February 1997, in St. Paul, Minnesota.
49. Meltzer, *Rescue*, p. 73.
50. David S. Wyman, *The Abandonment of the Jews: America and the Holocaust*. New York: Pantheon Books, 1984, p. 38.
51. Quoted in Hallie, *Lest Innocent Blood Be Shed*, p. 72.
52. Quoted in Hallie, *Lest Innocent Blood Be Shed*, p. 102.

Chapter 6: Denmark Saves Its Jews

53. Harold Flender, *Rescue in Denmark*. New York: Simon and Schuster, 1963, p. 32.
54. Quoted in Misser, *The Resistance*, p. 137.
55. Quoted in Meltzer, *Rescue*, pp. 93–94.
56. Flender, *Rescue in Denmark*, p. 63.
57. Flender, *Rescue in Denmark*, p. 75.
58. Elliott Arnold, *A Night of Watching*. New York: Charles Scribner's Sons, 1967, p. 177.
59. Quoted in Flender, *Rescue in Denmark*, p. 100.

60. Yehuda Bauer, *A History of the Holocaust.* New York: Franklin Watts, 1982, p. 11.

61. Quoted in Flender, *Rescue in Denmark*, p. 100.

Chapter 7: The United States and Resistance to the Holocaust

62. Bauer, *A History of the Holocaust*, p. 296.

63. Wyman, *The Abandonment of the Jews*, p. xii.

64. Quoted in Robert S. Ross, *So It Was True*. Minneapolis: University of Minnesota Press, 1980, p. 133.

65. Leni Yahil, *The Holocaust: The Fate of European Jewry, 1932–1945*. New York: Oxford University Press, 1990, p. 611

66. Quoted in Wyman, *The Abandonment of the Jews*, p. 43.

67. Quoted in Yahil, *The Holocaust*, p. 96.

68. Wyman, *The Abandonment of the Jews*, p. 182.

69. Quoted in Bauer, *Jews for Sale*, p. 317.

Chapter 8: The Jews of Hungary

70. Kati Marton, *Wallenberg: Missing Hero.* New York: Arcade, 1995, p. 67.

71. Andreus Biss, *A Million Jews to Save: Check to the Final Solution.* London: Hutchinson, 1973, p. 31.

72. Quoted in Yahil, *The Holocaust*, p. 518

73. Quoted in Timothy Bent, ed., *Wallenberg: Letters and Dispatches 1924–1944*. New York: Arcade, 1995, p. 230.

74. Quoted in Marton, *Wallenberg: Missing Hero*, p. 79.

For Further Reading

Elliott Arnold, *A Night of Watching*. New York: Charles Scribner's Sons, 1967. Exciting account of how the Danish people collectively organized the escape of the entire Jewish population of Denmark.

Andreus Biss, *A Million Jews to Save: Check to the Final Solution*. London: Hutchinson, 1973. The story of the attempt to save the Jews of Hungary and the work of the Budapest Committee of Jewish Assistance, who gave their lives in the effort.

Shalom Cholawski, *Soldiers from the Ghetto*. London: Nativity Press, 1980. The moving story of a ghetto survivor who escaped to the woods of Lithuania. Focuses on Jewish partisans and their contribution to the war.

Harold Flender, *Rescue in Denmark*. New York: Simon and Schuster, 1963. Easy-to-read account of how the Danes, assisted by the Danish underground, successfully sent nearly eight thousand Danish Jews to Sweden in 1943.

Anne Frank, *The Diary of a Young Girl*. New York: Washington Square Press, 1955. A moving diary of a young girl who spent two and a half terrifying years hiding from the Nazis in Holland. Her story is an expression of hope and joy for life.

Miep Gies, *Anne Frank Remembered*. New York: Simon and Schuster, 1987. The warm account of one of the people who worked to save the lives of the Frank family.

Joe J. Heydecker, *The Warsaw Ghetto: A Photographic Record 1941–1944*. London: I. B. Tauris, 1990. This volume of photographs of the Warsaw ghetto is an excellent entry into a lost world.

David Kahane, *Lvov Ghetto Diary*. Amherst: University of Massachusetts Press, 1990. Poignant account of how the Jews of Lvov rose against their Nazi oppressors.

Ruth Kluger and Peggy Mann, *The Last Escape: The Launching of the Largest Secret Rescue Movement of All Time*. New York: Doubleday, 1973. Story of Ruth Kluger, who, sent from Palestine, helped to organize transportation for Jews attempting to escape to Palestine.

Kati Marton, *Wallenberg: Missing Hero*. New York: Arcade, 1995. Well-written and sympathetic account of Raoul Wallenberg, his life, his appearance on the international stage, and his valiant efforts on behalf of the Jews of Budapest.

Milton Meltzer, *Rescue: The Story of How Gentiles Saved Jews in the Holocaust*. New York: Harper & Row, 1988. An excellent introductory account for students who seek to understand the efforts of people to save portions of the Jewish population of Europe.

Russell Misser, ed., *The Resistance*. New York: Time-Life Books, 1979. A story in text and photographs of some of the resistance groups that sprang up in Europe both to defeat the Nazis and to assist as many Jews as possible to escape the Holocaust.

Works Consulted

Yehuda Bauer, *A History of the Holocaust.* New York: Franklin Watts, 1982. A detailed discussion of the history of the Jewish people in Europe and how they became the object of the murderous designs of Adolf Hitler.

Yehuda Bauer, *Jews for Sale? Nazi-Jewish Negotiations, 1933–1945.* New Haven, CT: Yale University Press, 1994. A glimpse of the painful and largely futile attempts to find a way for tens of thousands of Jews to escape the Final Solution.

Yehuda Bauer, *The Jewish Emergence from Powerlessness.* Toronto: University of Toronto Press, 1979. A series of essays explaining how the lack of a national state rendered the Jews of Europe unable to gather together forces sufficient to resist the Holocaust.

Timothy Bent, ed., *Wallenberg: Letters and Dispatches 1924–1944.* New York: Arcade, 1995. This book contains a collection of lengthy official documents and letters written by Wallenberg and provides insight into his concerns and hopes.

Michael Berenbaum, *The World Must Know: The History of the Holocaust as Told in the United States Holocaust Memorial Museum.* Boston: Little, Brown, 1993. A poignant account of the Holocaust, told in pictures and text, produced in conjunction with the opening of the Holocaust Memorial Museum in 1993.

Asher Cohen, *The Halutz Resistance in Hungary.* New York: Columbia University Press, 1986. Story of how survivors from Poland and Slovakia played a central role in saving large numbers of Jewish children in Budapest and of awakening the Jews of Hungary to the danger confronting them.

Lucy S. Dawidowicz, *The War Against the Jews.* New York: Holt, Rinehart, and Winston, 1975. The book relates in great detail how Hitler and his collaborators set out to destroy the Jews as one of Germany's main war efforts.

Israel Gutman, *Resistance: The Warsaw Ghetto Uprising.* New York: Houghton Mifflin, 1994. Extremely detailed account of the efforts of the young resistance fighters to glorify the memory of their people by dying in their defense.

Philip P. Hallie, *Lest Innocent Blood Be Shed: The Story of the Village of Le Chambon and How Goodness Happened There.* New York: Harper & Row, 1979. An extremely emotional account of how an individual pastor and the congregation he led saved thousands of Jewish lives during World War II.

Raul Hilberg, *The Destruction of the European Jews.* Chicago: University of Chicago Press, 1961. Contains a great deal of information useful to the understanding of this extremely complex subject.

Robert Katz, *Black Sabbath: A Journey Through a Crime Against Humanity.* London: Macmillan, 1969. Discussion of how Italians dealt with the Jews under their jurisdiction, before and after the fall of Mussolini.

Isaac Kowalski, ed., *Anthology of Armed Jewish Resistance 1939–1945.* Brooklyn: Jewish Combatants Publishing House, 1992. A compilation of stories told by Jewish fighters during World War II. Includes many illustrations and photographs.

Dov Levin, *Fighting Back: Lithuanian Jewry's Armed Resistance to the Nazis, 1941–1945.* New York: Homes & Meier, 1985. Comprehensive account of the resistance of the Jews of Lithuania, in ghettos, in partisan groups, and in the Lithuanian division of the Soviet army.

Michael R. Marrus, ed., *The Nazi Holocaust: Jewish Resistance to the Holocaust.* Vols. 4 and 7. Westport, CT: Meckler, 1989. An enormous compilation of articles regarding all aspects of the Holocaust, written by the best-known scholars in the field.

Leon Poliakov, *Jews Under the Italian Occupation.* Paris: Editions Du Centre, 1955. Series of documents indicating attempts by the Italian army to prevent the Italian government from carrying out German demands to murder the Jews of Italy.

Robert W. Ross, *So It Was True.* Minneapolis: University of Minnesota Press, 1980. An account of how the Protestant press in the United States reported the events of the Holocaust to its readers.

Arnold Schoenbrun, *Soldiers of the Night.* New York: E. P. Dutton, 1980. The author worked for American intelligence in France during the war. He knew many of the members of the resistance, whose activities he describes in great detail.

Weapons of the Spirit, a documentary by Pierre Sauvage, 1989.

David S. Wyman, *The Abandonment of the Jews: America and the Holocaust.* New York: Pantheon Books, 1984. A thorough review of reasons behind the failure of the U. S. government to come to the assistance of Holocaust victims before 1944.

Leni Yahil, *The Holocaust: The Fate of European Jewry, 1932–1945.* New York: Oxford University Press, 1990. The author, an Israeli, provides an exhaustive account of events in Europe as they affected European Jews before and during World War II.

J. K. Zawodny, *Nothing but Honor: The Story of the Warsaw Uprising, 1944.* Stanford: Hoover Institutional Press, 1978. The story of the Warsaw uprising and the role of Jewish resisters from the ghetto.

Yitzhak Zuckerman, *A Surplus of Memory: Chronicle of the Warsaw Ghetto Uprising.* Berkeley and Los Angeles: University of California Press, 1993. The author, fighting under the name Antek, was one of the heroes and survivors of the Warsaw ghetto uprising.

Index

Picture Credits

About the Author

Deborah Bachrach was born and raised in New York City, where she received her undergraduate education. She earned a Ph.D. in history from the University of Minnesota. Dr. Bachrach has taught at the University of Minnesota as well as at St. Francis College, Joliet, Illinois, and Queens College, the City University of New York. In addition, she has worked for many years in the fields of medical research and public policy development.